ABOUT THIS BOOK

Thank you for purchasing this textbook. Philadelphia Press is a green, independent publishing company that specializes in creating texts and eBooks for today's college students. This book has been created especially for you! We worked with your professors to create a book that will help you take from this class valuable skills and knowledge that you will use throughout your academic career and life.

Public Speaking books are very expensive. The top book in the marketplace retails for over $200! We have made a very special effort to deliver you a textbook at an affordable price, without sacrificing quality. In addition, Philadelphia Press has a number of eco-friendly policies aimed at reducing our footprint in this wasteful industry

You will note that this book has multiple authors. They are all directors of speech programs at colleges and universities in the area, and provide their unique voices to the chapters that they wrote. In an effort to tailor the content of this book to match your course curriculum, some chapters have been altered by our editors. For a complete transcript of a specific chapter, please write to Philadelphia Press.

Lastly, we ask that you not sell back your book so that we may keep the price low. Used books are a way for the bookstore to make more money and the students are not paid fair prices for their used books. Please consider your fellow and future students and help us to establish a culture of low priced books.

Philadelphia Press is an eco-friendly, environmentally conscious company. We strive to keep our carbon footprint to an absolute minimum, and to deliver non-paper products whenever possible.

Books may be purchased for educational purposes.
For information, please call or write: (888) 851-3367

Philadelphia Press
7715 Crittenden St. #390 • Philadelphia, PA 19118
Web site: wwwphiladelphiapress.com • Email: info@philadelphiapress.com
ISBN 978-0-9974030-8-4
Printed in the United States of America

TABLE OF CONTENTS

1

The Role of Public Speaking

Dr. Tracey Quigley Holden
University of Delaware

Communication is a central characteristic of human beings; our brains are hardwired to develop language and seek social interaction. So it is not surprising that humans also have a long tradition of studying communication: how it works, what makes it more or less effective, and how we can improve our skills. In this chapter, you will read about some of the history and tradition of public speaking, key principles of thinking and listening that support effective communication, and the basics of the communication process. These core concepts will lay a strong foundation for you to build on as you develop your communication skills.

The Tradition of Public Speaking

The ancient Greeks are credited with some of the earliest formal studies of communication. More than two thousand years ago, philosophers you have probably heard of — Socrates, Plato, and Aristotle - spoke and wrote extensively about the **rhetoric** of public persuasion. Aristotle's book — *On Rhetoric: A Theory of Civic Discourse* (Aristotle, 1991), is still considered the most important book on rhetoric ever written (Golden, 2007). The **Sophists** were teachers and practitioners of rhetoric who offered instruction and gave extended public orations to demonstrate their talents. It's important to remember that Greek society depended on oral communication in many essential functions including government and court proceedings.

Pericles monument next to Ciy Hall in Athens, Greece

All citizens were expected to participate in public debates and discussions. A skilled speaker had a tremendous advantage. Alcidamas, an important Sophist, argued that public speaking was more challenging and more effective than written texts. Public speaking, he said, required the speaker to effectively communicate with their audiences in the moment, rather than taking time to reflect on and edit their words (Alcidamas, 2001). Alcidamas taught his pupils that they needed to be fully prepared on their topics so that they be able to respond to the audience in the moment of speaking. In many ways, Alcidamas was advocating for what we now term "extemporaneous speaking" and use of a "conversational tone" from the speaker. So even if the speaker has acquired significant knowledge and has thought carefully about what they want to say on a given topic, they must also, according to Alcidamas, recognize the needs of the audience and respond to those needs. A sense of mutual participation is at the core of excellent speaking. If both the speaker and the audience are contributing and engaged in the communicative process, it's far more likely that an effective exchange will occur. However, Alcidamas also lived in a time when significant changes were occurring in many aspects of communication, as the increasing use of written language and texts began to challenge the oral traditions. In fact, despite Alcidamas's claims, written texts and experts were becoming more important and more powerful in society. You might see some parallels to our contemporary society and changes in communication methods. The ancient Greeks were moving from a strong oral tradition to a more literary or written model; we are moving from the literary model to a more digital model. In both situations, changing communication practices and methods have advantages and disadvantages, not all of which can be predicted.

Although written texts certainly became more important, the influential role of public speaking continued, as it does to the present day. Roman scholars and statesmen valued public speaking and continued its study. **Cicero**, a Roman Senator and contemporary of Julius Caesar, developed the five essential Canons of Rhetoric as a guide to effective speech. They are **invention**, **arrangement**, **style**, **delivery**, and **memory**. **Invention** is what goes into a speech — the content and information it contains. **Arrangement** is the organization — how the content is structured and in what order. **Style** is how the information is presented — formally or informally, with ornate or plain language. Cicero held beautifully crafted, graceful, and polished speeches in high esteem; he believed that elegant style was a distinctive mark of excellence in a speaker. **Delivery** is the physical act of speech including gestures, movement, tone, pace, and inflection. **Memory**, which was added some time after the first four Canons, is the process of learning and memorizing a speech. The principles of the Canons endure, with some adjustments for our contemporary usage. Delivery is now often linked to what medium or channel is used to deliver the message as much as to the physical delivery. Memory for speakers today often refers to what elements make the speech memorable or distinctive for both audience and speaker rather than to the process of memorization.

The Five Canons of Rhetoric

1. INVENTION
2. ARRANGEMENT
3. STYLE
4. DELIVERY
5. MEMORY

Approaches to Public Speaking: Ancient Egypt

The origins of rhetoric, and by extension public speaking, are largely rooted in Western thought; however, over the last two decades scholars have sought to incorporate recognition and understanding of classical rhetorical legacies outside of Greece and Rome. This is particularly important as we consider the rapid demographic shifts we are seeing in the United States as it relates to an increase in students of color and the multiculturalism of the student population. *African American Rhetoric(s): Interdisciplinary Perspectives* (2007) by Ronald L. Jackson and Elaine B. Richardson, states:

> As we enter a new century of scholarship in interdisciplinary fields, many of us have finally come to appreciate and to understand critical advantages in having theoretical frames that take into account achievements that may and may not resonate with European cultural traditions. In broadening our horizons with experiences and information from different geographical and cultural spaces, we extend our horizons and enrich our understanding, not just of peripheral people in knowledge-making arenas but of human potential.

Much work has and continues to build a base to inform public communication practices and scholarship drawing from ancestral Africa. Early work by Molefi Kete Asante, has created the baseline of work connecting the symbols, motifs, and language practices of ancient Egypt to the current practices of diverse cultures, such as African-Americans. Asante is the author of several books, including but not limited to, *Kemet, Afrocentricity and Knowledge,* and *Rhetoric, Race and Identity: The Architecton of Soul* (2005). From these works including, the works of others, we know that the Egyptians valued reticence, believing that language should not be used carelessly, and that silence can and was used strategically. These concepts are laid out in ancient Egyptian texts called sebyt (sebait), which means "instructions". Thus, according to Fox (1983), the Five Canons of Kemet (ancient Egyptian) rhetoric are:

- **Silence:** The act of self control as a way to maintain your good reputation.
- **Good timing:** Be deliberate when you speak, so as to stay distinguished yourself.
- **Restraint:** Be aware that the heart may contain words that should not be said aloud, as speaking is more dangerous than fighting.

- **Fluency:** You must give the impression of confidence, security and stability when you speak.
- **Truthfulness:** Honesty creates your character and it is in itself, persuasive.

For ancient Egyptian teachers, these Five Canons together encompass what Western thought would call **ethos** (appeal to ethic and good character). The **ethos** created by the aforementioned canons of Egyptian rhetoric is that of harmony with divine justice. There is a fundamental association between the Egyptian instructions and those of Quintilian in their emphasis on the **orator** (person speaking) rather than on the **oratory** (what is being said). Egyptian rhetoric can be encapsulated in Quintilian's dictum that only a good man can speak well (Fox, 1983).

Much of classical ancient Egyptian rhetorical practices have been used in examining, understanding, and studying African-American oratory, communication dynamics, and practices. Outside of the Five Canons of Kemetic Rhetoric, African classical rhetoric values communalism, **nommo** (the power of the word), building community, dignity, and eloquence.

Significance of Diverse Approaches to Public Speaking

As you study and practice the art of public speaking using this text, it is important to consider the origins of rhetoric, not just from a Western perspective, but also from a multiplicity of approaches. This will allow you, as a student, to discover a broader understanding of public address and engage with intellectual treatments that are not limited in scope or geographical region. Culture-centered approaches to rhetoric live outside of Rome and Greece as well as Egypt. According to *The Culture of Speeches: Public Speaking Across Cultures* (1997) by Mary R. Power and Camille Galvin, public speaking taught in Australian universities to local students and to students from Asian countries advises students from a Western approach. However, the article notes, this way of speaking does not take into account the multicultural audience and it adheres to an implicit assumption that there is but one way of communicating in public—that given to us by rhetoricians in Greece and Rome who set the "rules" for public speaking. Students of intercultural communication can find that scholars such as Gudykunst and Kim (1992) suggest that the rhetorical tradition of Europe and North America reflects not a universal communication style but rather the cultural patterns of logical, rational, and analytic thinking favored in those countries (See: Power & Galvin, 1997).

As we learn to consider the multiculturalism of our audiences, as well as the culture of speakers, it is important to address communication strategies that are both productive and unproductive. Productive communication strategies tend to unite diverse audiences, while unproductive strategies are divisive, inefficient, and polarizing.

Although there are many more significant contributors to the tradition of communication, these early scholars and practitioners built a foundation that we rely on today. The central role of communication in community life and in the pursuit of knowledge is well established by the Greeks, as is the importance of teaching communication as an essential life skill adaptable to changing times. The Romans kept communication at the center of public and political action, and incorporated key aspects of ethics, public service, and the role of the citizen. Our complex, globally connected, and technologically advanced world has not seen any reduction in the need for strong, creative communication skills based on these foundations more than 3000 years later! In fact, you will see in the next section that we have added a few specific applications of communication skills needed to navigate today's world.

Critical Thinking and Listening as Communication Skills

Much of our discussion and instruction around communication focuses on messages and messengers. But if we return to the foundations of public speaking, the first canon is invention — careful consideration and evaluation of the content of our speeches. Knowing what facts to include and what to leave out is a key part of effective, ethical communication. Senator Daniel Moynihan is credited with the saying, "Everyone is entitled to their own opinion, but they are not entitled to their own facts" (Moynihan, 2010). We live in a society swamped with information, with very little distinction made between fact, fiction, opinion, and fabrications. In 1982, Buckminster Fuller reported that human knowledge had doubled about every century prior to 1900. Since the beginning of the 20th century, that pace has rapidly increased and only shows signs of accelerating. A decade ago, IBM scientists claimed that by the mid-21st century, the Internet of Things could be doubling our knowledge every 12 hours (IBM Global Technology Services, 2006). As we try to manage life and make decisions in the midst of all of this information, two key but often underdeveloped and underused skills become essential — critical thinking and critical listening.

Critical thinking is an active process which requires self-reflection and assessment of our own tendencies, biases, and pre-conceptions along with the information we consider. With over 4.5 billion pages on the indexed Web, more than 500 direct broadcast channels, nearly 2,000 television stations, and over 1,000 newspaper in the U.S., access to information is almost unlimited; but the quality and accuracy of all the information varies wildly. Developing our abilities to evaluate, interpret, analyze, explain, and regulate our preconceptions allow us to function more effectively (Tillius, 2012). The saying, "Knowledge is power" only holds true when the knowledge we hold is accurate and usable.

If critical thinking skills are underdeveloped and underused, the ability to listen critically is on the endangered list. Not only is listening rarely taught or practiced, but our culture values multi-tasking and multiple inputs in ways that diminish our capacity to listen. You probably know someone who does homework with a television on, or can't seem to walk across campus without talking on their phone or listening to music.

Critical thinking is the ability to thoughtfully and carefully gather, assess, and use information to improve understanding, refine our beliefs, and guide our actions.

Critical listening shares many qualities with critical thinking — the incorporation of careful attention, comprehensive checking, and applying reason to what we hear.

If critical thinking poses significant challenges for us, critical listening adds another level. We have become accustomed to high levels of distraction and low levels of attention. Practicing good listening takes concentrated effort and focus. Not only do we need to use our critical thinking skills to discern the differences between facts and mere assertion, we also need to be able to check assumptions; does the speaker offer support for their claims, or do they merely make unfounded statements? Accepting claims without evidence makes for easier listening, but less reliable information. Finally, we need to maintain a reasonable level of openness to new ideas.

When we hear ideas or information that contradicts our existing knowledge, we experience **cognitive dissonance**. It takes effort to evaluate the new information, check to see if it can be connected to what we already know, and then incorporated into new, usable knowledge. Finally, along with openness to new ideas, critical listening requires that we refrain from pre-judging a speaker. **As with critical thinking, our own biases and pre-conceptions can cause us to reject accurate and valuable information from a speaker simply because they don't conform to our existing understanding.** Critical thinking and critical listening set standards for speakers and listeners — both strive for accuracy, understanding, and increased knowledge. How that happens is the focus of the next section.

The Speech Communication Process

As much as history can (and should) inform our current understanding of the world we live in, it's an imperfect and often misdirected record. Early speech communication analysis was influenced by information processing models, developed by engineers working for Bell Laboratories — the telephone company. Claude Shannon and Warren Weaver developed a model to determine the information capabilities of transmission equipment. The model offers an elegant view of the communication process, but leaves out nearly all of the confounding human factors. Shannon and Weaver didn't need to consider the faults and foibles of humans in their model. From the most basic perspective, it does provide some clarity about the following: how communication happens, what can interfere with the communication process, and the idea of options for sending messages.

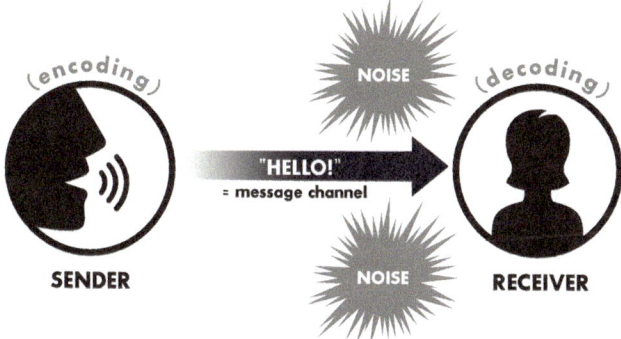

Figure 1.1
SOURCE: Jones, R. (2016). Communications in the Real World: An Introduction to Communication Studies, v. 1.0 Flat World Education

The sender has an idea, crafts a message into language (encoding), and sends the message to a receiver. The receiver decodes the message and then can send a response back to the sender. Noise is anything that interferes with the message transmission or receipt; it can be literal noise, distraction, lack of comprehension, or a host of other possibilities. [Figure 1.1 and 1.2]

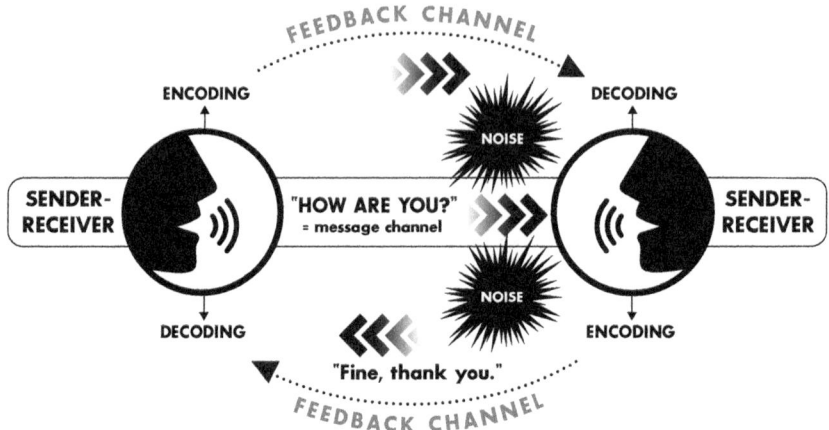

Figure 1.2

SOURCE: Jones, R. (2016). Communication in the Real World: An Introduction to
Communication Studies, v. 1.0: Flat World Education

One way to think about this process is as continuous feedback. Feedback in the
model is communication responding to an initial message, but it's much more
active than that. All of the participants are responding to the interaction and giving
feedback, at all times, and feedback can be verbal or non-verbal. Speakers who
notice the feedback from their audiences can adjust their presentations to be more
effective. Negative non-verbal feedback can include a bored or unhappy facial
expression, frowning, head shaking, crossed arms, leaning back, or even turning
away from the speaker. Negative verbal feedback can include disapproving
sounds like "nah" or "no" or comments that are combative, disapproving, or
heckling. Positive non-verbal feedback often includes smiling, nodding, leaning
forward, and looking interested; positive verbal feedback can be as simple as
a "yes" or even an "uh-huh" or more extensive, like a follow up question or
supportive comment. Good speakers and listeners pay attention to the feedback
in their interactions and use it to make their messages more effective.

The problems with this basic model are significant. Communication simply doesn't occur in a neat, one-at-a-time, linear way. In many ways we are always communicating; we don't stop conveying meaning when we stop speaking. Perhaps more importantly, we bring our full selves into every communication situation or interaction. Our understanding of the context, the participants, the intentions for this particular interaction, the possible outcomes, and our own history and experience to that very moment all influence how, what, and when we communicate. And it all happens at the same time!

Modes of Delivery

MEMORIZED SPEECHES — In Ancient Greece it was not uncommon for public speakers to recite their speeches from memory. Though memorizing a speech is a less familiar practice today, this impressive mode of delivery can still be very effective. However, you have to make sure to rehearse thoroughly and have the speech down 'cold.' Otherwise, the effectiveness of the speech can take a back seat to a disengaged delivery as the speaker focuses more on recalling words and phrases than on reaching the audience.

MANUSCRIPT SPEECHES — Sometimes a message is so important that its every detail must be recounted perfectly. A speaker can cover all their bases accurately and effectively by reading from a precisely worded, prepared manuscript. Examples of this mode of delivery include a President's address to Congress, a political figure's acceptance of a nomination, and a valedictorian's speech at a college commencement. Transforming the written word into a dynamic and powerful speech is an art form unto itself, requiring skill, hard work, and rehearsal. A speaker must learn to balance his or her attention between reading the words on the page and looking up and making eye contact with the audience at the appropriate time. Make sure your manuscript is legible. When delivering the speech, avoid a cold reading and a monotone voice. The trick is to convey the full and detailed message of the speech with a natural, sincere demeanor to which the audience can relate.

IMPROMPTU SPEECHES — These are speeches made with little to no preparation. They will probably make up the bulk of your experiences speaking in public. In fact, day-to-day conversing is a kind of impromptu speaking. With no prior notice, you may be asked or compelled to speak in a classroom setting, business conference, or in response to a preceding speaker. This is no cause for alarm. No one expects the Gettysburg Address in such a situation. Staying calm, listening, and maintaining awareness of what's going on and what's being said will definitely come in handy when you are faced with making an impromptu speech.

EXTEMPORANEOUS SPEECHES — This type of speech is carefully prepared and rehearsed but is not written down word for word, giving the speaker the ability to adjust to the present situation and connect with the audience in a direct conversational way. In giving the speech, the speaker will refer to concise notes, elaborating on them in a fresh natural manner. This form of delivery is a great way to keep your speech sounding spontaneous no matter how many times you rehearse. The illusion of conversation provided in this form of delivery can help to put the audience at ease and make them more receptive to your message.

In Conclusion

In this chapter we have covered a lot of ground, from the early Western traditions and foundations of communication, to key cognitive skills needed for effective communication and a first look at communication processes and models. Each of these elements connects to and informs the others. Furthermore, we have seen that what we have learned from the ancient rhetoricians still holds currency today. Perhaps because communication is such a central aspect of humanity, perhaps because communication pervades our culture and society, the lessons learned thousands of years ago continue to teach us today.

References

Alcidamas. (2001). Alcidamas: *The Works and Fragments.* (J. Muir, Trans.)
Briston: Bristol Classical Press.

Aristotle. (1991). *On Rhetoric: A Theory of Civic Discourse.* (G. A. Kennedy, Trans.)
Oxfort: Oxford University Press.

Everitt, A. (2001). Cicero: *The Life and Times of Rome's Greatest Politician.* New York:
Random House.wGolden, J. L. (2007). The rhetoric of Western thought: From the
Mediterranean world to the global setting. Dubuque, IA: Kendall Hunt.

IBM Global Technology Services. (2006). *The Toxic Terabyte.* London: IBM UK.

Moynihan, D. P. (2010). *Daniel Patrick Moynihan: A Portrait in Letter of an
American Visionary.* (S. R. Weisman, Ed.) New York: Public Affairs.

Plato. (2008). *Gorgias.* (R. Waterfield, Ed.) Oxford: Oxford University Press.

Quintilian, M. F. (1969). *Instution Oratoria.* (G. A. Kennedy, Trans.) London:
Twayne Publishers.

Tillius, G. (2012, June). *Six Critical Thinking Skills You Need to Master Now.*
Retrieved from Rasmussen College: http://www.rasmussen.edu
student-life/blogs/main/critical-thinking-skills-you-need-to-master-now/

Walzer, A. E. (2001). Quintilian's "Vir Bonus" and the Stoic Wise Man.
Rhetoric Society Quarterly, 25-41.

2

The Role of Ethics

With Contributions from **Dr. Sheena Howard**
Rider University

Imagine a world where you could do or say whatever you were thinking, where you could use your actions or powers of speech purely to further your own gain or destroy the credibility of another without fear of reprisal. Think of the damage you could do to others, the world, and, for that matter, yourself. Fortunately, laws and moral codes have been put in place over time to help keep people on the path of doing and saying the right thing. These moral codes are known as **ethics** and they are a crucial part of public speaking.

In the sphere of ethical public speaking, we generally adhere to the following rules:

- Speak Ethically

- Listen Ethically

- Be Respectful to others and considerate of their gender and ethnicity, also their physical and mental disabilities

- Don't Plagiarize

Speak Ethically

Remember the power that you have as a speaker. Make sure that your goals are morally sound. Do not mislead your audience.

Listen Ethically

Always extend the same courtesy to a speaker that you would have extended to you. Of course it is never acceptable to heckle a speaker, but even talking to a friend during a speech or failing to pay attention are also forms of disrespect.

Plagiarism

Plagiarism occurs when a speaker or writer presents someone else's work or idea as their own. This includes failure to properly cite sources of intellectual property or academic research. There are different types of plagiarism that you will learn about in this chapter. Most universities have very strict policies regarding plagiarism, and there are extreme consequences for violating those policies.

Remember that the written and spoken word are powerful forms of communication that can have a great effect on people and ideas. That's why it's always important to be mindful of the ethical significance of the words we choose when writing and delivering our speeches. See below for Camden County College's Academic Honesty Policy.

CAMDEN COUNTY COLLEGE ACADEMIC HONESTY POLICY

Academic Honesty Guidelines

CHEATING AND PLAGIARISM

All students are expected to do their own work. All forms of academic dishonesty are absolutely forbidden. Students who cheat, plagiarize, or commit other acts of academic dishonesty will be subject to immediate disciplinary action. This may result in an automatic grade of 'F' for an assignment and/or for the course. Academic dishonesty may also be subject to additional penalties as determined by the College in accordance with sanctions for violations of the *Student Code of Conduct*.

Academic Dishonesty Definitions:

The following are examples of academic dishonesty but not the full range of prohibited behaviors in the classroom, studio, laboratory, library, testing center, computer center, internship placement, or any other sites.

1. Cheating is defined as an act of deception by which a student misleadingly demonstrates that he or she has mastered information on an academic exercise. Behaviors that will be considered cheating include but are not limited to:

   a. Unauthorized copying or allowing another to copy a test, examination, quiz, paper, project, or performance;

   b. Using or attempting to use unauthorized materials (such as notes, books, computer-based media, formula lists, "cheat sheets" or a computer translator in a foreign language assignment) during a test or out-of-class assignment;

   c. Communicating during a test in any way with anyone other than the test administrator using paper, cell phones, text messaging, or other media;

   d. Submitting a paper, a project or major portions of a paper or project that have been previously submitted in another class without the permission of the current instructor;

   e. Turning in a written, oral, or computer-based assignment that is not the student's own (including labs, art projects, homework, prewritten or purchased papers, or work downloaded from the Internet);

   f. Improperly obtaining a test or any information about a test;

   g. Stealing, buying or otherwise obtaining all or part of tests or other academic materials belonging to a faculty member;

   h. Changing, altering or being an accessory to the changing or altering of a grade in a grade book, on a test or any official academic record of the college that relates to grades;

i. Forging or altering attendance records;

j. Intentionally impairing the performance of other students, such as by adulterating laboratory samples, creating a distraction, or altering computer files.

k. Taking a test for someone else or permitting someone to take a test for you; and

l. Intentionally using invented information or falsified research as authentic findings.

2. Plagiarism is defined as the act of representing the work of another as one's own without proper citation. Behaviors that will be considered as plagiarism include but are not limited to:

a. Failing to give credit, using acceptable academic methods for written, oral or computer- based ideas or materials taken from others;

b. Representing another's artistic or scholarly work as one's own;

c. Using another's analogy, algorithm, code or style to produce a computer program;

d. Using another's data, solutions, computer accounts, or calculations without the appropriate authorized permission; and

e. Listing sources on a works-cited page or in a references list that were not actually used.

ACADEMIC DISHONESTY CONSEQUENCES AND APPEALS

Consequences

1. Faculty members may impose academic penalties for academic dishonesty at their discretion.

2. This could include assignment of make-up work, a grade of F for an assignment or for the course, etc.

3. Students who are assigned a grade of F for a course as a penalty for academic dishonesty will forfeit their right to withdraw from the course.

4. Students who are accused of academic dishonesty may be referred to the executive dean of enrollment and student services for disciplinary action.

5. Academic dishonesty is considered a violation of the *Student Code of Conduct* and is subject to the same procedures and sanctions as any other misconduct.

Appeals

A student desiring to appeal the penalty imposed for academic dishonesty must follow the College's outlined general academic appeal procedures or disciplinary appeal procedures, depending on whether the penalty was imposed by a faculty member (general academic appeal) or by student services, including the Hearing Board (disciplinary appeal).

The Ethics of Public Speaking

The National Communication Association is the most influential communication association in the United States, with a membership of more than 8,000 communication scholars and practitioners (Abbott, Timmerman, McDorman & Lamberton, 2016). In 1999, the association published its *Credo for Ethical Communication* that outlines ethical communication behaviors in the public and private spheres of communication. This credo provides a great overview of the implications and practices of ethics across the field of communication.

NCA Credo for Ethical Communication

(approved by the NCA Legislative Council, November 1999)

Questions of right and wrong arise whenever people communicate. Ethical communication is fundamental to responsible thinking, decision making, and the development of relationships and communities within and across contexts, cultures, channels, and media. Moreover, ethical communication enhances human worth and dignity by fostering truthfulness, fairness, responsibility, personal integrity, and respect for self and others. We believe that unethical communication threatens the quality of all communication and consequently the well-being of individuals and the society in which we live. Therefore we, the member of the National Communication Association, endorse and are committed to practicing the following principles of ethical communication:

We advocate truthfulness, accuracy, honesty, and reason as essential to the integrity of communication.

We endorse freedom of expression, diversity of perspective, and tolerance of dissent to achieve the informed and responsible decision making fundamental to a civil society.

We strive to understand and respect other communicators before evaluating and responding to their messages.

We promote access to communication resources and opportunities as necessary to fulfill human potential and contribute to the well-being of families, communities, and society.

We promote communication climates of caring and mutual understanding that respect the unique needs and characteristics of individual communicators.

We condemn communication that degrades individuals and humanity through distortion, intimidation, coercion, and violence, and through the expression of intolerance and hatred.

We are committed to the courageous expression of personal convictions in pursuit of fairness and justice.

We advocate sharing information, opinions, and feelings when facing significant choices while also respecting privacy and confidentiality.

We accept responsibility for the short- and long-term consequences for our own communication and expect the same of others.

Source: National Communication Association. Credo for Ethical Communication.1999.https://www. natcom.org/uploadedFiles?About_NCA/Leadership_and_Governance/Public_Policy_Platform?PDF-Policy Platform_NCA_Credo_for_Ethical_Communication.pdf

As you can identify in the qualities described by the National Communication Association credo, the following are important as it relates specifically to ethics and public speaking:

- Honesty and accuracy
- Actively and empathetically listening before responding
- Access to communication resources
- Positive contributions to the well-being of humanity through communication
- Creating a climate of mutual understanding
- Focus on unity and communalism, despite varying perspectives and viewpoints
- Courage in expression
- Accountability and responsibility for speech acts

The aforementioned list may be helpful in understanding the nature of ethics and public speaking. Though it is not always clear how one can practice the ethics of communication as a student of public speaking, such a practice is often made more apparent by our pre-existing ethical standards. Ethical standards, or moral principles, are the set of rules we abide by that help us distinguish good from bad and right from wrong in our thinking and actions. (Millner and Price, 2016).

In the next section, we will use the foundational criteria established here to provide concrete tactics for incorporating ethics into the process and delivery of public communication messages. Incorporating and understanding ethical practices of public speaking will not only make you a better speaker but also shield you from the possible embarrassment of consequences related to unethical public communication. These consequences could include removal from one's job, loss of friendships, being shamed and smeared via social media, and failing a college course.

The Practice of Ethics in Public Speaking

As a public speaker you should always be aware of the power, responsibilities, and consequences that come with addressing an audience. Below are some core ethical public speaking ideas and behaviors that you should consider.

The First Amendment

Congress shall make no law respecting an establishment of religion, or prohibiting the free exercise thereof; or abridging the freedom of speech, or of the press; or the right of the people peaceably to assemble, and to petition the Government for a redress of grievances.

Under the First Amendment freedom of speech is guaranteed except in certain instances. These instances include hate speech, support of terror, slander, false threats, true threats, and false advertising among others. As a public speaker it is important to be aware of when you are crossing the line between legal and illegal speech.

Ethical Speaking: Scrupulous Self Examination

In the course of researching, preparing, and presenting you should continuously make sure that you are complying with both ethical and legal standards. Whether the speech is informative, persuasive, or commemorative, scrupulous self examination is your best protection against making an error that is embarrassing or worse.

Plagiarism

Plagiarism is using someone else's work or ideas without giving the source credit or acknowledgement. When it comes to public speaking, we often become inspired by speeches and ideas by others. Naturally we wish to incorporate some of these good elements into our own work. In fact, this practice is both welcome and encouraged. However, using someone else's idea or work always requires you to cite its source. To avoid plagiarism do not submit work (an outline or speech) that is not your own. In addition, do not try to deliver a speech that was already written or delivered by someone else.

There are three distinct types of plagiarism — global, patchwork, and incremental plagiarism (Lucas, 2011). According to Millner and Price, **global** plagiarism, the most obvious form of plagiarism, transpires when a speaker presents a speech that is not his or her own work (Millner and Price, 2012). **Patchwork** plagiarism is plagiarism that occurs when one "patches" together bits and pieces from one or more sources and represents the end result as his or her own (Millner and Price, 2012). Michael O'Neill (1980) also coined the term "paraplaging" to explain how an author simply uses partial text of sources with partial original writing. The third type of plagiarism is **incremental** plagiarism. This occurs when most of the speech is the speaker's original work, but quotes or other information have been used without being cited. An example of incremental plagiarism would be providing a statistic to support your claim, but not providing the source for that statistic (Millner and Price, 2016).

Ethical Listening

Some of the early Greek and Roman philosophers – Aristotle, Socrates, and Plato — spoke extensively about morality and ethical principles. Just as there are ethical practices when it comes to speaking, there are also ethical practices when it comes to listening. In an article titled, *Listening for Diversity* (2016), Sally Lehrman outlines four ethical ways news reporters can listen ethically as it relates to understanding the values of marginalized communities. She cites the following ways to better your listening by employing an ethical approach.

- Quiet your mind. Don't assume your definitions are the same as your sources.

- Ask why? Look for the story behind the story. Listen for the reason behind the statement.

- Meet your source where she/he is, both literally and figuratively. You'll be able to hear better if you are in your source's comfort zone, not your own. And she/he will be more forthcoming.

- Ask what your source actually does, not just what he thinks and knows.

Lehrman's ethical approach to listening shows us that audiences have a responsibility, which involves a process of listening beyond simply hearing or receiving sound bites. It is the responsibility of the listener to acknowledge fairness and accuracy in the way they interpret and disseminate information. From a news reporting perspective this cannot be done without practicing ethical listening as outlined above. Think about the ways in which you can improve your communication skills by simply incorporating these ethical listening guidelines into both your public speaking and interpersonal relationships. All of the guidelines laid out here can be improved upon by being polite and attentive, avoiding prejudging the speaker, and maintaining the free and open expression of ideas.

Accountability and Respectability

One way to engage in ethical public speaking practices is to set responsible speech goals in which you maintain accountability for the consequences of your public communication. This process should begin as you prepare your speech and should continue through to its delivery. To be accountable means to consider your audience and the ways in which your presentation will affect them. Considerations such as inclusive language, avoiding hate speech, assuming responsibility for raising social awareness, and employing respectful speech are all responsible speech goals that you should consider (Millner and Price, 2016). In addition, you should be aware of the ways in which you appeal to the emotional fears and concerns of your audience (to the detriment of logical appeals). Be careful not to use false or unsound arguments — fallacies to support claims throughout your speech.

As you move on to chapters on *Research, Speech Structures,* and *Outlining,* use the guidelines in this chapter to inform your research and delivery decisions. Starting out with good habits, such as ethical listening, ethical research, productive public speaking qualities, and understanding the history of diverse approaches to communication, you develop "best practices" early on in your learning process. As we have noted in this chapter, this will be beneficial in your personal, professional, and public life.

References

Abbott, J., McDorman, T., Timmerman, D., & Lamberton, L. J. (2015). Public Speaking and Democratic Participation: Speech, Deliberation, and Analysis in the Civic Realm. Oxford university press.

Asante, M. (1990). Kemet, Afrocentricity, and Knowledge, Trenton: Africa World Press

Asante, M. (2005). Rhetoric, Race, and Identity: The Architecton of Soul. Amherst, NY: Prometheus Books

Fox, M. (1983). Ancient Egyptian Rhetoric, Rhetorica, (1, Spring):9-22.

Gudykunst, W.B. & Kim, Y.Y.(1992). Communicating with strangers:

an approach to intercultural communication. (2nd ed) New York: McGraw Hill. History of Public Speaking. (2016, May 26). Retrieved June 6, 2016, from Boundless website: https://www.boundless.com/communications

Hutto, D. (2002). Ancient Egyptian Rhetoric in the Old and Middle Kingdoms. Rhetorica: A Journal of the History of Rhetoric, 20(3), 213-233. doi:1. R trieved from http://www.jstor.org/stable/10.1525/rh.2002.20.3.213 doi:1

Lehrman, S. (2016). Listening for diversity. Quill, 104(2), 38.

McKay, B., & McKay, K. (2011, January 26). Classical Rhetoric 101: The Five Canons of Rhetoric â€" Invention. Retrieved June 5, 2016, from the art of manliness website: http://www.artofmanliness.com/2011/01/26/classical-rhetoric-101-the-five-canons-of-rhetoric-invention/

Millner, A., & Price, R. (2016, March). ethics in public speaking. Retrieved June 7, 2016, from Public speaking project website: http://www.publicspeakingproject.org

Lucas, S. E. (2001). The art of public speaking (7th ed.). New York: McGraw-Hill.

O'Neill, M. T. (1980). Plagiarism: Writing Responsibly. Business Communication Quarterly, 43, 34-36.

Power, Mary R. and Galvin, Camille (1997) "The culture of speeches: Public speaking across cultures," Culture Mandala: The Bulletin of the Centre for East-West Cultural and Economic Studies: Vol. 2: Iss. 2, Article 2.

Richardson, E. B., & Jackson, R. L. (2007). African American rhetoric (s): interdisciplinary perspectives. SIU Press.

Schulz, P., & Cobley, P. (2013). Theories and Models of Communication. Berlin: De Gruyter Mouton.

Williams, K. (2012). Improving fear appeal ethics. Journal of Academic and Business Ethics, 1-24. Retrieved June 05, 2016, from http://www.aabri.com/manuscripts/11906.pdf

Witte, K. (1992). Putting the Fear Back into Fear Appeals: The Extended Parallel Process Model. Communication Monographs, 59(4), 329-349.

Witte, K. (1993). Message and Conceptual Confounds in Fear Appeals: The Role of Threat, Fear, and Efficacy. The Southern Communication Journal, 58(2), 147-156.

Witte, K. (1994). Fear Control and Danger Control: A Test of the Extended Parallel Process Model (EPPM). Communication Monographs, 61(2), 113-134.

3

Speech Anxiety: Problems and Solutions

Dr. Tracey Quigley Holden
University of Delaware

One of the most common feelings associated with public speaking is anxiety — sometimes called stage fright, nerves, or just plain fear of public speaking. Comedian Jerry Seinfeld has joked that people in the United States are more afraid of public speaking than death – so much so that at a funeral they would rather be the deceased than give the eulogy! Yet there are some people who are quite comfortable speaking to a large group, but who feel anxious at a party, in meetings, or in one-on-one situations like interviews. Scholars in communication are well aware of the phenomenon and in research have found that people experience anxiety in many communicative situations, not just public speaking. More than forty years ago, Dr. James McCroskey labeled this common feeling "communication apprehension" and began developing measurements and scales for assessing the anxiety felt in many communication situations (McCroskey, 1970). But even a hundred years ago, teachers and practitioners of public speaking had been discussing how to manage stage fright and feelings of anxiety associated with communication. In this chapter you will learn about communication apprehension and how to manage it in ways that help you communicate more effectively, no matter how you are feeling in the moment. "Feel the Fear and Do It Anyway" was the title of a popular book in 1987 that quickly showed up on bumper stickers and posters and was used as a motivational quote by many people. More practically, it can be a personal mantra and a little extra push for facing and managing communication apprehension.

Glossophobia, Social Phobia, and Social Anxiety Disorder

In 2013, Google marketed a tablet as a research and education tool for K-12 students. In its advertising, it showed a middle school boy searching for "glossophobia", which Google defined as the fear of public speaking. Indeed, many if not most people experience feelings of anxiety and stress when asked to give a public speech. In fact it is estimated that 75% of all people have some degree of anxiety/nervousness when public speaking (Hamilton, 2013). Those feelings are uncomfortable, but not to the point of causing people to avoid giving speeches entirely.

Glossophobia and social phobia, however, are types of social anxiety disorder, a recognized mental health condition. The Mayo Clinic defines social anxiety disorder to include "fear, anxiety and avoidance that interferes with your daily routine, work, school or other activities" (Mayo Clinic, 2017). These conditions can contribute to, but are distinguishable from the communication apprehension described earlier. Social anxiety disorder is characterized by intense and persistent feelings of fear of humiliation, fear of judgment, fear of failure, and anxiety that seem uncontrollable. They can cause people suffering from them to avoid a wide range of social situations, even when such avoidance is personally or professionally costly. It is estimated that about 7% of the U.S. population suffers from a social anxiety disorder (National Institute of Health, 2017). Glossophobia is a performance-related anxiety. People with performance anxiety may not have difficulty in social situations, but instead feel anxious when called on to give public speeches or other forms of performance, such as dancing or playing music, sports competitions, or taking a test. There are very effective therapeutic and medical treatments for social anxiety disorder and for performance anxiety.

Knowing about 7% of people have to deal with social anxiety, let's consider that in the context of a typical public speaking class of 20-30 students, that's about 2 people who are affected. For most students, the anxiety and stress they feel before giving a speech is normal, manageable communication apprehension. That's what made the Google ad so effective; it showed that good information and preparation could reduce anxiety. There is a predictable, physical response to the need for your body and brain to take action. Knowing what that is and how it works is what the next section is all about.

The Betrayal and Benefit of Biology

In order to understand and manage your communication apprehension, it helps to know something about human biology and the production of fear. It is well known that the human brain and body are wired to respond to stress of any kind with a "fight or flight" response. In the early twentieth century, Walter Cannon identified the response and began research on the physiological causes and effects in humans. There are two parts to the response, produced by different areas of your brain.

When we experience stress of any kind, our brains and bodies produce a response geared to help us either fight or flee from the situation. One concept which helps us understand brain function is the "triune brain" (Maclean, 1990) or three general brain parts with specific functions. While this is widely acknowledged to be a gross oversimplification of brain structures, it does give us a way to conceptualize brain activity. So the brain stem and cerebellum handle automatic, reflexive behavior – basically the things you should not spend time thinking about, like breathing and keeping your heart beating. This is sometimes called the reptilian or "lizard brain", as it is arguably the oldest part of our brains, essential to life, but lacking the ability to reason. The limbic system, including the amygdala, handles emotional responses but at the gut level – it feels, but does not think. The cerebrum and neocortex form the larger part of your brain, and they handle memories, planning, and thinking in general. So in the FIRST response to stress or strong emotions, your "lizard brain" signals the body to produce extra quantities of several hormones, including adrenaline and cortisol. Your limbic system contributes intense feeling and heightened awareness. Adrenaline heightens the muscular response and glucose available for immediate action, while cortisol suppresses the immune system and converts fatty acids to energy.

The lizard brain and limbic system are boosting all your available systems to give you maximum energy. Unfortunately, this hormonal and emotional activity tends to have some unpleasant side effects, such as increased heart rate, a feeling of flushed skin, cold hands and feet, the feeling of your throat constricting, butterflies in the stomach, shaking or trembling of your muscles, and others. The side effects and what is noticed in a stress response vary from person to person, but the physiology is almost identical.

Your brain perceives a need for energy and enthusiastically dumps hormones into your system to provide it. But your lizard brain, the part of your brain that manages these responses, doesn't have rational thought capabilities—it doesn't care if you are seeing a saber toothed tiger or giving a two minute speech. Instead, it works on a stimulus-response basis. Got stress? Get energy! Your lizard brain and limbic system together can act a lot like a toddler with a box of cookies and no adult supervision, grabbing as much as they can from the box as fast as they can. The result is a system overload and overreaction driven by physical and emotional reactions. This is the betrayal of our biology—our lizard brains and limbic systems have no ability to think. When your thinking brain, the neo-cortex, finally kicks in, it can help to assess and manage the thoughtless responses of your lizard and limbic systems. A key part of the thinking brain's job is to identify and label – give words to – our physical and emotional responses. This is the SECOND response, and it can lag well behind the first response. Your thinking brain starts analyzing the situation using language to describe and label the key pieces. Your thinking brain can tell the toddler to have one cookie, notices that there is NO saber toothed tiger in the area, and recognizes that the audience of your peers is actually pretty harmless. That's the benefit of biology! If you were actually in danger, your lizard brain would have given you a quick response to save your skin. If there is no imminent danger, your thinking brain can usually take over, label the situation, and use the energy to produce an appropriate response.

From the beginning, it is important to understand that the physical and emotional feelings you may have are driven by your brain and body trying to give you energy to cope with perceived stress. *The physiology is the same, no matter what kind of stress you are experiencing.* This is where our thinking brain and our use of language can be a huge benefit. In our SECOND response, when we think, we can assess the situation accurately and manage our physical and emotional response effectively. A key part of this process is to recognize the feelings for what they are – a response to stress, the creation of extra energy — and label them in ways that help us act effectively. Thinking is done with language. We cannot think about something until we name it, so we can use naming to help us manage the response.

Imagine for a moment that you are getting ready to go to a party. You're within minutes of departing, and everything is going well. You're rushing just a bit to be ready on time. You know that good friends will be there, the party is well-planned with fun things to do, and even the weather is cooperating. As you grab your keys and head for the door, how do you feel?

Here's another scenario—you are getting ready to go take an exam. You've studied hard, but you're just not sure you really understand all the material. A big part of your grade depends on this test, and a lot of your classmates have been texting about how they're studying – some have been up all night. You got some sleep, you've had a good breakfast and an extra cup of coffee, and you think you're ready. As you grab your keys and head for the door, how do you feel?

Most likely for the first scenario, you imagined feeling excited, happy, and eager to get to the party. In the second situation, you probably imagined feeling anxious, stressed, and reluctant to go take the test.

Guess what? Your brain and body are responding to each of these stress situations with extra adrenaline and emotional intensity. The difference is that in the first scenario, your mind is labeling those responses and feelings with words like "happy" "excited" and "anticipation". In the second, your mind is grabbing different labels like "anxious" "stressed" and "worried". You are interpreting the same physical and emotional responses in your brain and body differently. In both situations, your brain and body are responding to stress with the same physiological actions, while your mind is applying different words.

If you understand that the physiological response is just energy, and that you can choose how to label it, you are well on your way to being able to manage your communication apprehension!

The next section will discuss effective techniques for relabeling, reducing, managing, and even benefiting from the communication apprehension you experience.

Managing Communication Apprehension

Once you understand the biology of apprehension, you are in a much better position to get your thinking brain in gear and focused on mitigating the intense response of the lizard brain and limbic system. In addition to managing your involuntary brain and body responses, there are a variety of exercises and techniques that will help you boost your confidence and focus. There are, for example, several things you can do to manage communication apprehension, starting well before your actual presentation.

Prepare (don't procrastinate)

Normally, you have some time to prepare before you have to give your presentations. The single most effective thing you can do to reduce your communication apprehension is to prepare your presentation thoroughly and well ahead of the due date. Taking the time to really know and understand the topic you will be speaking about, finding and organizing high quality information, and planning your presentation carefully for both the audience and the time available are all essential to giving an excellent presentation. As a bonus, every aspect of preparation also reduces communication apprehension. The more familiar and comfortable you are with your material and your plan for presentation, the more confident and less apprehensive you will feel. Ideally, you would know the content of your speech so well that delivering your message is almost effortless – instead, you can focus on the response from the audience and adapting your message in the moment. When it comes to public speaking, procrastination is one of your worst enemies. Procrastination leads to stress, which can amplify your feelings of apprehension. Even if you feel that some spontaneity or inspiration is lost in the process, the advantages of thorough preparation of your materials far outweigh the disadvantages of leaving preparations until too late.

Figure 3.1 **Ways To Manage Communication Anxiety**

- **Prepare (Don't Procrastinate)**
- **Practice**
- **Use Your Thinking Brain (Relabel and Rename)**
- **Use Your Body (Release, Redirect, Reframe)**
- **Focus on the Needs of Your Audience**

A second significant and helpful aspect of thorough preparation is that it allows you to focus on crafting the most effective message for your audience. It may surprise you that the message your audience needs to hear may not be the same as the one you'd like to deliver! Thinking through the likely composition of your audience members and some key elements of their current knowledge of your topic is essential to building and delivering a truly effective speech. Ask yourself, "What does my audience know, feel, or understand about this topic? What do I want them to know, feel, or understand after my presentation?" By focusing on the needs of your audience, you accomplish three things. You create a speech that contains the information most likely to add to what your audience already knows in a positive way. You shift the focus of the speech from yourself and your message to the audience and their communicative needs, which will reduce your concerns about being judged on your performance. Finally, focusing on audience needs always improves a presentation, because people enjoy feeling that you are giving them something "just for them." When you are able to do that, their opinion of you as a speaker goes up, too.

Practice

Once you have the content and organizational plan for your presentation, practice is crucial. Moving from the written pages or notecards you have prepared to effective delivery to an audience takes practice, if only because what is written down does not always sound right when spoken aloud. Multiple rehearsals of your presentation will help you recognize the places where your speech flows smoothly, where you are comfortable with the material, help you identify the spots that need polishing or need a note or reminder. An additional benefit of multiple rehearsals is desensitization. Systematic desensitization is a psychological technique used for many fears and phobias. Exposure to a smaller level of the stimulus that provokes fear or anxiety in a controlled situation helps you to reduce your stress response. Over time your brain learns that stimulus X does not pose a significant threat, and your stress response decreases. When you practice giving your presentation, especially if you either imagine your audience there, or actually have someone watch you, you are simulating the stress of the actual presentation but at a reduced level. By engaging in the behavior that your brain perceives as stressful in an environment which is more comfortable for you, you become 'desensitized' to the situation. The more often you practice, the more your brain recognizes the situational cues correctly and gives you just the energy you need, instead of going to full alert.

Use Your Thinking Brain (Relabel and Rename)

Even with thorough preparation and practice, you are likely to still feel some communication apprehension. As discussed earlier, this is a normal physiological and emotional response of your brain and body to any form of stress. You can still use your "thinking brain" to help you manage both your physical responses and the emotional feelings of stress. First, new research from Harvard Business School shows that recognizing the emotional feelings of stress and relabeling them more positively can "flip the switch" of your experience (Brooks, 2014). Excitement is the emotional twin of apprehension. Both involve some uncertainty in anticipation of action, but our labels are different. The technique used at Harvard is simple—as you notice the feeling of apprehension, you say out loud, "I am excited!" or "Get excited!" Instead of perceiving the situation as a threat, you relabel your perception to see it as an opportunity. That perceptual switch helps you relabel your feelings, switching from apprehension to excitement. The bonus of relabeling is that it also improves performance. Participants in the research who relabeled with "I am excited!" or "Get excited!" were scored higher by observers. When study participants were tasked with giving a speech, the participants who said "I'm excited!" out loud scored higher on persuasiveness, persistence, competence, and confidence. Those are pretty positive qualities for any speaker!

If switching from apprehension to excitement seems a bit of a stretch, or if you want an added boost for your performance overall, you can rename your physical responses. The technique is similar to relabeling, but focuses on identifying and

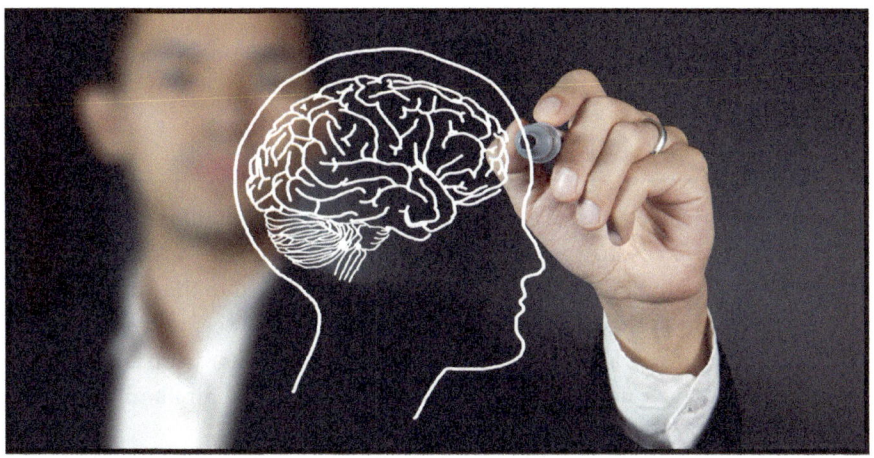

directing the physical responses of your body as energy for your performance. The first act of our thinking brain is to find words for the feelings produced by the reptilian and limbic systems. Our words, especially those used for responses associated with emotions, have both denotative and connotative meanings. The denotative meanings are the dictionary definitions, the core meaning of the words. The connotative meanings are the additional interpretations imposed on the word by our experiences. For example, we all agree that "cat" has a denotative meaning of four legged mammal of the feline species. For someone who loves cats, 'cat' carries many other positive connotations — love, warmth, pleasure, purring. For a person who is not so fond of cats, 'cat' might carry connotations of scratching, hissing, witches and bad luck. Neither connotation is wrong, but they are definitely different. Thus the words we use to name something bring their own connotations along with the core meanings. Recall our discussion of the lizard brain's contribution of adrenaline and cortisol. Both hormones act to maximize the energy available to you and the speed of your responses. By naming the physiological response as energy, your thinking brain helps to diminish the emotional aspect of the response and the connotations that are associated with whatever words you might have named those emotions. Energy is what we all need to accomplish the tasks on our to-do lists. Identifying and renaming your physical response as energy helps you direct that positivity toward your presentation.

These techniques can be used separately or together. Relabeling and renaming the physical and emotional response to stress does take some thinking effort, and a certain level of awareness of your own responses to stress. For some people, it is easier to relabel the emotional response; for others, renaming the physical response as energy is easier. There is no right or wrong way to use these techniques – try both and see what works for you.

Use Your Body (Release, Redirect, Reframe)

When we experience stress, it is not unlikely that someone will tell us to "Keep Calm and Carry On" – borrowed from the famous British World War II poster. It is worth knowing that those posters were never distributed to the British people. They were kept in storage, to be used only in the worst case scenario of a German invasion. The phrase was intended to help Britons endure hardship and extreme circumstances which might go on for a long time. "Keep Calm and Carry On" may sound like an effective way to manage unavoidable stress or anxiety, but it is very difficult to do in the moment. When your brain and body are in "fight or flight" stress response mode, calming down is an impractical goal. Instead, by realizing that the physical response to stress creates an abundance of energy in the human body, you can find ways to release or redirect that energy. You can also use your body to create a physiological response that will help you perform better.

One technique is to release some of the extra energy you have. The easiest way to release it is to burn it off. If you have a choice between taking a few flights of stairs or taking the elevator, take the stairs. If you can walk around a bit, do so. If you have to stay in one place, squeeze your hands into fists and open them a few times, or tap your feet on the floor. Shrug your shoulders up and down. Indeed, move in any way you feel comfortable moving in a controlled way. As you burn off the energy, your sense of intensity and anxiety will diminish as well.

Another technique to use is so simple and quiet, it can be done anywhere – just breathe. Oxygen is a great antidote to anxiety. Your body is ready to respond to any perceived threat with fight or flight, and part of that reaction is an increased heart rate and faster breathing. Those shallow, quick breaths cut down on the oxygen available in your system and heighten your feeling of tension. Taking a deliberately slow, deep breath, holding it for a second or two, and releasing it slowly, helps your body reset itself, and to know that it is not immediately threatened. That deep breath actually uses some of the energy being used to speed up your systems, and using the energy acts as a counter to the adrenaline boost in the system. Adding oxygen to the mix also tells your brain and body that you are not at immediate risk. Taking a deep breath also gives your thinking brain time to take a little more control of the situation. It is a little like pushing a reset button. Once you have taken a good deep breath (or two) you can reassess your situation and take action to help your performance.

Releasing your extra energy should still leave you with more than you need to give your presentation. This is where the redirection of your energy can help you. Elite athletes, musicians, and other creative people spend hours practicing their skills, but many of them also use visualization for specific elements of their performance. A third technique, active visualization, helps redirect your energy into creating the actions you need to perform. Tennis players will visualize every motion of a perfect serve, golfers a perfect swing, musicians see themselves perfectly producing every note. Redirecting your energy through visualization teaches you what you need to do to perform successfully – it is a form of mental rehearsal of the physical performance. A short visualization of yourself successfully giving your presentation channels your energy into reproducing that success. As you visualize your movements, gestures, and "see" yourself giving a great speech, you are simultaneously teaching your body and brain how to recreate it in real performance. Another visualization technique is called the Bubble. For the Bubble you imagine yourself inside a lovely bubble, which smells and feels like your favorite place in the world. While in your bubble you start your presentation, and the bubble expands to include all of your audience members. Giving your speech is effortless! After you conclude, your bubble shrinks down to just enclose your body, and you can float happily along through your day. The Bubble also redirects your energy into your audience connection and your message, and away from your reactive state of apprehension.

The final technique for managing communication apprehension actually does quite a bit more than just help with a presentation. Dr. Amy Cuddy at Harvard Business School conducted research on the effect of particular physical positions of the body for people giving short presentations. The study showed that people who adopted "high power poses" for periods of two and five minutes prior to their presentation were evaluated more positively, and their presentations were given better ratings, than people who adopted "low power poses" for the same periods of time (Cuddy, Wilmuth and Carney, 2012). Cuddy's research (and her TED talk—see QA code below) explain that our senses of confidence and competence are affected by the way we hold our bodies. High power poses are expansive and take up more space; they increase feelings of dominance, action, risk-taking and increase pain tolerance. High power poses also reduce stress and anxiety – as you will recall reducing stress and anxiety is the key to managing communication apprehension. One way to use this research is to simply hold a power pose for a few minutes, shortly before your give your presentations. The high power poses Cuddy used in her research are pictured here.

But more than just boosting confidence and reducing stress for a presentation, Cuddy suggests that power posing can alter how we behave across many situations, which fundamentally reframes how we act. As Cuddy says in her TED talk, "Our bodies change our minds, and our minds change our behavior, and our behavior changes our outcomes." Power posing increases our action orientation, so we are more likely to do or try something new. At the same time, power posing seems to foster positive evaluations from others. The combination of the two can act to reframe how we see ourselves in the world: as more competent and powerful. Competent, powerful, action-oriented people might still feel anxiety and apprehension, but they are not going to let that get in their way. There is too much to do on the way to their goals!

Your body language may shape who you are | Amy Cuddy

Remember to Focus on the Needs of Your Audience

One final technique you can use to cope with anxiety is to focus your attention on the audience, on what they need from you as a speaker, and how they respond to what you say. Think of your speech as part of a conversation in which you are presenting ideas to your listeners. The more you internalize this dynamic, the less nervous you will be and the more your message will resonate.

Conclusion

In this chapter, we have discussed the challenge of communication apprehension, how the brain and body produce it, and how our brains and bodies can help us manage and reduce it. We also distinguished communication apprehension from glossophobia and social phobia. It is important to remember that nearly every speaker experiences some form of communication apprehension. Recognizing the effects of communication apprehension from both psychological and physiological perspectives is the key to effective management. Preparation and practice can reduce anxiety before your presentation. åRelabeling and renaming techniques can be used in the moment of your presentation. Releasing, redirecting and reframing before, during, and after your presentation to shape your experience and your response. Communication apprehension isn't going away, but it won't keep you from speaking up!

References

Brooks, Alison W. (2014). "Get Excited: Reappraising Pre-Performance Anxiety as Excitement." Journal of Experimental Psychology, 143(3) pp 1144 – 1158.

Cannon, Walter (1932). Wisdom of the Body. United States: W.W. Norton & Company.

Cuddy, Amy J.C. (2013) Your body language shapes who you are. https://www.ted.com/talks/amy_cuddy_your_body_language shapes_who_you_are?language=en

Cuddy, Amy J.C., Caroline A. Wilmuth, and Dana R. Carney. (September 2012) "The Benefit of Power Posing Before a High-Stakes Social Evaluation." Harvard Business School Working Paper, No. 13-027.

Hamilton, C. (2013). Communicating for Results, a Guide for Business and the Professions (tenth edition). Belmont, CA: Thomson Wadsworth.

Jeffers, Susan. (1987) Feel the Fear and Do It Anyway. New York: Random House Publishing.

MacLean, Paul D. (1990). The triune brain in evolution: role in paleocerebral functions. New York: Plenum Press.

McCroskey, J. C. (1970). "Measures of Communication-Bound Anxiety." Speech Monographs, 37(4), 269.

4
Informative Speaking

Dr. Matthew Jones
County College of Morris

The Function, Purpose, and Goal of the Informative Speech

Broadly considered, there are three types of speeches: (1) Informative Speeches, (2) Persuasive Speeches, and (3) Commemorative Speeches. Although the general purpose of a speech has traditionally fallen into one of three categories: (1) Speeches to Entertain, (2) Speeches to Inform, and (3) Speeches to Persuade

The general purpose of a speech is defined by its central idea. If the central idea refers to a "lesson," the speech is informative: whereas, if it refers to a "proposition," the speech is persuasive. The central idea of commemorative speech is the person, people, or event being celebrated.

In this chapter, we will discuss the most common type of speech—the informative. The purpose of an informative speech is of course to provide information to an audience, but it helps to think a little beyond what can sometimes seem like a dry recitation of facts and figures. Informative speeches at their best increase both the speaker's and the audience's understanding on a given topic. The facts and figures are selected, arranged, and shared in a way that provides context and relevance for the knowledge gained. Considering an informative speech from the perspective of increasing understanding can help you focus on a topic and on what to include to best reach that goal.

Choosing a Topic, Specific Purpose and Central Idea

In most classes on public speaking, you are assigned a particular type of speech to give, including the general purpose of the speech. Many students struggle to find a good topic, sometimes getting caught up in wondering "Will the instructor like it ? Will the audience think it's boring ?" Whether your speech has been assigned to you or you are faced with another kind of speaking situation, you should take yourself into consideration. After all, you will be the one giving the speech and your success as a speaker will be based on your relationship to the topic you have chosen. If you don't have at least some interest in your topic, it makes it much more difficult to communicate effectively to anyone else. As you decide upon a topic and work out the specific purpose of your speech, consider not only what you want your audience to know, but what you are most interested in sharing.

To be a good speaker, you must find your own authentic voice. Doing this requires careful examination of your own experiences, interests, and talents from the perspective of the application they might have to audiences. If you can identify something you're good at, that you enjoy and have a lot of experience with, and that other people would benefit from learning, then you're on the right track. Of course, most speeches are not about your personal interests or experiences, but finding a connection between your experience and your topic is a key step toward a good speech.

Use the table below to identify unique and important experiences you've had that relate to your interests and talents. Once you've done this, start to consider how these experiences, interests, and talents might be applied to a topic. The stronger the relationship that exists among these four items, the more likely it is that you have found your authentic topic.

Experiences	Interests	Talents	Application

A *specific purpose statement* refers to the particular intentions of the speaker within the broader context of the generalized informative or persuasive purpose.

It is stated as an infinitive phrase and includes the general purpose, a reference to the audience, and the objective of the speech. It should focus on one topic, making sure it is not worded vaguely nor is too broad of a topic such that it can be covered in the time frame allotted for the speech. Be sure to use clear and concise language, eliminating any figurative language. The specific purpose statement will be reworded to be audience-centered and is used in the Introduction of the speech to accomplish the objective "reveal topic."

Examples of Specific Purpose Statements for Informative Speeches

1. **To inform my audience on how a tornado develops**

2. **To inform my audience about the history of telephones**

3. **To inform my audience about diabetes**

The specific purpose statement identifies the objective of the speech whereas the *central idea* summarizes the ideas of your speech in order to fulfill the objective stated in the specific purpose statement. It is comparable to a thesis statement or a subject sentence in a written essay.

The central idea usually starts to take shape after you have done some research and have decided on the main points of your speech. The main ideas of the speech should be reflected in the central idea in the same order as you present them in the body of the speech. It may be changed slightly as you develop the body of your speech so as to accurately reflect your main points. Sometimes the central idea will even incorporate the actual wording of the main points.

Since the central idea concisely identifies the main ideas of your speech for your audience it also is reworded to be audience-centered and is used in the Introduction to "preview the speech" and in the Conclusion to "summarize the main points" (Chapter 7). It is written as a single, declarative sentence using concrete words and language that is familiar to your audience. As mentioned above for the specific purpose statement, you want to also avoid using language that is figurative or ambiguous.

Analysis of your Audience

Once you've examined your own experiences, interests, talents, and the ways that they can be applied, the next step is to think about your audience. In public speaking, it's not possible to think about each audience member as thoroughly as you think about yourself, so you need to consider more efficient ways of learning about them.

One way you can get to know your audience is by studying their **demographics.**

Demographics are qualities specific to a group that include age, sex, gender, race, nationality, regionality, ethnicity, culture, sexual orientation, and other variables.

Related to demographics, sometimes it is possible to consider **psychographics** as well.

Psychographics is the study of people's activities, interests, and opinions, aimed at understanding their attitudes and values.

Psychographics are more difficult to assess than demographics, but there are times when information about your audience can give you some insights. If you know that a significant portion of your audience belongs to a particular organization or engages in a shared activity, that can help you understand their attitudes and values. For example, speaking to a group of Habitat for Humanity volunteers would suggest attitudes of altruism and valuing of community service.

Another way you can learn something about your audience is through their motivation: why did they show up? Maybe you're presenting a theory at an academic conference, or addressing graduates at a commencement ceremony, eulogizing at a funeral, or giving a toast at a wedding. In these scenarios and the multitude of others that are possible, something about the audience is revealed just based on their presence at the speaking event.

Through demographics and motivation, you might be able to make some guesses about the experiences and knowledge of your audience, as well as their attitudes, beliefs, and values (more on this in Chapter 5). This is important because learning is incremental, which is to say, we learn new things based on what we already know. So when presenting an informative speech, it's important to know about the experiences and knowledge of your audience.

Classifying Informative Speeches

Informative speeches are typically categorized as speeches of…

1. **Description**

2. **Explanation**

3. **instruction**

Speeches of Description

Speeches of Description focus upon and seek to illuminate the features of an object, person (or animal/plant), place, region, period of time, experience, emotion, or anything else at all that's capable of being experienced through senses, thoughts, or feelings. Broadly stated, speeches of description attempt to answer questions that ask "what" (not how or why) insofar as inquiry centers on what features or aspects compose the thing that is being described. The objective of a descriptive speech, therefore, is to create a mental image in the mind of the listener of what is being described.

Imagine, for example, that you went on a camping trip with a group of friends. There would be a variety of ways to describe camping. You might focus on the features of the campsite, camping tasks, or outdoor activities that one can do, or wildlife that might be encountered.

Once you've settled on a *specific purpose*, you can start to consider the central idea and main points of your speech. Let's say you want to focus on the "features of the campsite." The central idea of your speech could take the form of a lesson about the geography of a campsite. Phrased specifically, it might appear like this: *"You can learn a lot about the local environment from a camping trip."* From this point, you can start to identify features of the campsite that can be placed into categories and used as main points. In this example, where you are focusing on physical terrain, a spatial approach to organizing your main points might be used. Otherwise, a topical approach might be employed as in the following:

I. **The climate varies depending on where one goes on a camping trip.**

II. **Rock formations vary depending on where one goes on a camping trip.**

III. **The flora varies depending on where one goes on a camping trip.**

Speeches of Explanation

Rather than descriptions of features meant to develop mental images in the mind of the listener, a *Speech of Explanation* is concerned with meanings, origins, or correspondences. In short, a Speech of Explanation answers questions about "why" and "how" instead of "what" (i.e. when "what" refers to the thing being described). Keep in mind, though, that some level of description may be essential to a precise explanation, since explanation itself focuses on the correspondences between or among things. For example, if you are trying to explain how photosynthesis works, some description of plants, sunlight, carbon dioxide, water, chlorophyll, and oxygen will be necessary. Thus, an explanatory speech is primarily concerned with the relationships among things, particularly inasmuch as cause and effect are concerned.

Returning to the camping trip, what type of explanatory speeches might come out of such an example? The brief allusion to photosynthesis above could provide a useful starting point, especially since specific plant species might come in handy as examples for explaining the process. Additional possibilities might include explanations of moon phases, the food chain, the water cycle, fossils, or any other phenomenon that one might be exposed to in a wilderness setting.

Let us say for our present purposes that "photosynthesis" will serve as the topic of your explanatory speech. The Central Idea could be stated as follows: Photosynthesis is a process divided into two stages by plant biologists. Once the central idea has been determined it is then possible to identify Main Points and decide upon an organizational strategy that will inform the order of their presentation.

In this example, chronological strategy would be used to determine the order of main points. For example:

I. The first stage is the light-dependent reaction.

II. The second stage is the light-independent reaction or dark reaction.

Speeches of Instruction

In their most basic sense, *Speeches of Instruction* are intended to teach, that is, to transfer knowledge from speaker to listener. Like *explanation,* instruction is primarily aimed at answering questions of *how*, although, as in all informative speeches, other types of questions might be addressed along the way as well. This is especially true when aspects of description and reporting are applied to the task of instruction.

However, unlike any of the other types of informative speech described earlier, speeches of instruction are meant to develop competency in the listener. Consequently, understanding or comprehending the speech and remembering it are prerequisites for the development of other skills the speaker wishes to instill. Though, it should also be acknowledged that comprehension and memory are also skills in and of themselves.

According to Bloom's Taxonomy (a chart of verbs that describe different learning outcomes), other competencies fall under the following categories: *knowledge, comprehension, application, analysis, synthesis, and evaluation.* Particularly important among the many verbs that describe learning outcomes is *demonstration.* It goes without saying that to instruct effectively, one must possess the competencies necessary to demonstrate the skill being taught. For example, a math teacher needs to be able to demonstrate how to solve an algebra problem before expecting the student to solve it. It is through demonstration that the student is able to modify their own approach to achieve competency in the skill being taught.

Going back once again to our camping trip example, a number of possibilities should come to mind when considering how camping might be *instructed.* Everything from choosing a campsite and setting up equipment to essential skills like building a fire and cooking could take the form of an instructional speech. Depending on how ambitious the trip is, other more advanced skills like hunting, fishing, rock climbing, rafting, etc. might come into play as well. For our purposes, let's pretend we're going to give an instructional speech on how to set up a practical campsite. The main points below demonstrate one approach that might be taken:

I. The first thing to do when arriving at a camp site is to survey the area for the placement of the tent.

II. The second decision to be made is to find a location to set up the kitchen area.

III. Lastly, for socializing in the evening, a camp fire is a must.

Methods of Organization

Organizing Your Informative Speech

The most important principle to consider when organizing your informative speech is *complexity*. The "Principle of Complexity" dictates that information be presented in an incremental, hierarchical fashion that proceeds from simple to complex. Ideally, an informative speaker should begin right about at the limits of the audience's knowledge and present new information in stages, consistently relating it to the audience's existing base of knowledge. Some more specific strategies include the following:

- **CHRONOLOGICAL:** The chronological strategy is taken from storytelling, wherein events build upon each other successively, creating dramatic tension and resulting in a climax from which the moral of the story might be drawn. This strategy could be applied to a speech intended to inform about biographies, historical periods, technical procedures, or the subjective discovery process of the speaker.

- **SPATIAL:** The spatial strategy uses place, space, and/or geography as a tool of organization. Such a strategy could be applied, for example, to an informative speech identifying zip code as a predictor of poverty, wherein spatial relationships between cities were used to describe economic disparities in physical terms. Spatial strategies might also be employed to explain complex systems (such as a power grids or computers), communication patterns, and relationships between objects, ideas, or people.

- **CAUSE AND EFFECT:** The cause and effect strategy uses a sequence of related events as an organizing system. With cause and effect, it is critically important to establish the actual link between the events and the relationship — you cannot claim that Event X was the catalyst for Effect Y just because X happened before Y. When used correctly and effectively, the cause and effect organizational pattern is a powerful explanatory framework. To extend the example about poverty from the spatial pattern, a cause and effect approach might look at food access and nutrition as an underlying cause of poverty. Children who are undernourished often struggle in school (cause) — low school achievement often results in underemployment and cyclical poverty (effect).

- **COMPARE AND CONTRAST:** The compare and contrast strategy uses a structure of parallels as its primary organization. For each major idea or aspect of the topic, an alternative idea is presented and the similarities and differences discussed. Such a strategy could be applied to an informative speech about college options, where there are two or more choices available. The speech could focus on a few key aspects of college, such as academics, location, and campus life, comparing the similarities and contrasting the differences between campuses. A key aspect of this approach is to ensure relatively equal consideration given to each option, so as not to bias your audience.

- **TOPICAL:** The topical strategy has no predetermined relationship among main ideas, rather it allows the speaker to impose his or her own logic on how the speech is organized. It is especially critical in the case of a topical strategy that the speaker be conscious of the principle of complexity, since it is very easy to introduce information out of context and confuse the audience.

Conclusion

The ability to effectively convey information is crucial to our personal and professional lives. No matter what type of informative speech you are preparing, or what organizational pattern you choose, keep in mind the overall purpose of informative speaking. As a speaker, think about what your audience would most benefit from knowing and understanding about your topic. Whether you are helping to teach an old friend to tie a bowtie or presenting a production plan to a board of directors, informative speaking skills are critical to successfully conveying your message. You will probably be asked to present or evaluate an informative speech at some point during your public speaking course. In this chapter you have learned about different types of informative speeches, and about strategies for organizing an informative speech.

5
Persuasive Speaking

Dr. Matthew Jones
County College of Morris

Persuasion is the double-edged sword of public speaking; it can bring together the very best in effective communication, and it can demonstrate the very worst. At its best, excellent persuasive speaking can move audiences and speakers toward the highest ideals and efforts of human ability. At its worst, persuasive speaking can twist and manipulate ideas and push us toward evil actions. Persuasive speech is intended to influence the audience toward the speaker's desired response. In some situations, that response is an action by the audience; in others, acceptance of an idea or a change in attitudes toward a given subject. It is sometimes claimed that all communication is persuasive because all communication seeks to influence the audience in some way. There is some truth in that perspective, but here we will focus on persuasion that is intended to move an audience to mental or physical change desired by the speaker.

Before reading about how Purpose, Topic, Central Idea, and Audience relate to persuasive speaking, you may wish to revisit these sections at the beginning of the Informative Speaking chapter since they share a common foundation.

Central Idea, Purpose & Topic

Central Idea

The central idea for a persuasive speech always comes in the form of a proposition that the speaker shares with the audience at the start of the speech so that they have a context for interpreting the presentation and a clear sense of the speech's primary message.

Purpose

For any proposition of fact, value, or policy speech, the general purpose is always persuasive, that is to persuade listeners to believe or behave in a certain way.

Two minor clarifications are necessary regarding propositions and persuasion. First, it may occur to you that many statements made in the course of an informative speech may also appear as propositions based on the definition above. To some extent this is true, and we should remember that the boundary between informative and persuasive speaking is not absolute. Second, it should be noted that persuasive speaking isn't exclusively about changing people's minds. The definition above stipulates that the purpose of a persuasive speech is to "convince or reinforce" a proposition because some audience members will agree with your proposition from the start. In those cases, the purpose of the speech is to reinforce their agreement. Other members of the audience may be easily convinced; still others will require more effort to convince, and some will simply never be convinced no matter what you say or do. Persuasion can also be used to influence someone's perspective about a topic. Your speech may not lead to total agreement but if you are able to move people toward your point of view you are still being persuasive.

Therefore, we may define the General Purpose of a persuasive speech as such: *to convince or reinforce a Proposition in the mind of the audience.*

A proposition is the statement of an idea that may be accepted or rejected by an audience and is subject to debate.

Topic

Now that we've introduced Central Idea and Purpose in a persuasive context, let's revisit Topic as it applies to persuasion. You may recall from the informative chapter that to *be a good speaker you must find your own authentic voice,* and this means determining a subject area that you have *experience with, interest in, and talent for.* At this point, you should revisit that list in conjunction with the research and other material from your informative speech to determine how you might extend or contribute to that topic.

Adapting to the Audience

In the informative speaking chapter, you read about how you can make certain limited assumptions about the experiences and knowledge of your audience based on demographics, psychographics, and motivation. It was also briefly mentioned that these factors offer insight into *attitudes, beliefs, and values* which are three important concepts in persuasion.

While it is critical to recognize that one can never predict attitudes, beliefs, and values with total accuracy, it is equally important to learn how to be sensitive to these factors when crafting an argument. First, let's define these terms:

ATTITUDE: Positive or negative orientations

BELIEF: Perceptions of truth or falsehood

VALUE: Convictions about right and wrong

Generally speaking, we are least committed to our attitudes, and most committed to our values. Beliefs gravitate toward the middle of the spectrum with moderate levels of commitment. As a consequence of this hierarchy, it tends to be easiest to persuade people to change their general attitudes, but very difficult to persuade them to change their longstanding values. One way to think about the connection between persuasion and your audience's attitudes, beliefs, and values is to imagine how a lever works to lift a weight. Attitudes are the lever – they're relatively easy to determine and influence. Beliefs are like the weight on the end of the lever - it requires some effort to move them, and you need to get the lever (attitudes) moving first. Values are like the fulcrum – they're what supports everything else, and very difficult to move without a significant upheaval.

Ethos/ Logos/Pathos

In addition to presenting perhaps the oldest model of communication, Aristotle was also the first to closely analyze the art of persuasion *(rhetoric)* by dividing it into three qualities: *ethos, pathos, and logos.* Ancient as these principles are, they still describe the three major variables that contribute to or detract from the effectiveness of a persuasive appeal.

Ethos

Ethos refers to spirit or character. A large part of the persuasive effectiveness of a message comes from the person who is presenting it. To test this idea, think about how you would respond to surprising information shared by a close friend whom you trust versus an acquaintance with a hidden agenda who has lied to you in the past. The very same words would likely be treated seriously in the first case and with great skepticism in the second. We know, therefore, that the reputation of the communicator plays an important role in the persuasive effectiveness of the message.

Credibility

Credibility refers to the trust an audience places in the speaker, and it plays an important role in developing the sort of character audiences find persuasive.

In practice, credibility is an evolving mixture of reputation and performance—what you've done in the past and what you're doing now. Every performance is simultaneously a risk to and opportunity for one's reputation. Some theorists therefore divide credibility into three categories: *initial* (reputation), *derived* (earned during the performance), and *terminal* (the final impression of the speaker).

So what makes you trust a speaker? There are six primary qualities that enhance credibility: sameness, reputation, personal stakes, empathy, knowledge, intelligence, and personal experience.

Characteristics

- **SAMENESS:** For many reasons people tend to place more credibility in those who are similar to themselves. Noted communication theorist Wilbur Schramm also pointed out that we can only communicate to the extent that we share similar *fields of experience.*

- **REPUTATION:** As referenced above, reputation is a critical factor in establishing credibility, but it's not just about performance. Collective evaluation also plays an important role in shaping reputation. In other words, what counts is not just your performance, but also how the audience collectively interprets and evaluates your performance. Thus, it's especially important to consider the audience when crafting a persuasive speech.

- **PERSONAL STAKES:** What do you have to gain or lose with the success or failure of your persuasive appeal? The more clearly and obviously your personal stakes overlap with the collective stakes of your audience, the greater your credibility will be. Think about how you would feel, for instance, if a stranger gave you a gift. You might be grateful, but also skeptical about what they expect in return or could potentially gain from it.

- **EMPATHY:** The ability to relate emotionally to your audience is important for establishing trust and credibility. Do you care about the things they care about? If you do, they will put their faith in you and your credibility will increase.

- **KNOWLEDGE:** The more knowledge you have of the facts related to your persuasive appeal, the greater your credibility will be when speaking on your chosen topic. If it becomes apparent that you lack important knowledge associated with your topic, audiences will have reason to doubt you. For example, someone giving a speech about the history of the alphabet would lose all credibility if they attributed the first alphabet to a language like English or Russian. This is why it's important to choose a topic that you are interested in and willing to study carefully, including careful selection and citation of your sources.

- **INTELLIGENCE:** Intelligence refers to the ability to manipulate knowledge to achieve specific outcomes. Without intelligence, knowledge is meaningless and without knowledge, intelligence is vacuous. The audience will judge your intelligence on many factors, but foremost among them are the way you use language, your logic and reasoning, and your conclusions.

- **PERSONAL EXPERIENCE:** As discussed in the chapter on informative speech, science has changed how we have come to know the world through specialized methods used to overcome the natural limitations of personal knowledge. However, we still place great importance on individual personal experience, and for good reason. Personal experience is the intimate testing ground for all theory. If something lacks the resonance of truth in our own experience (or in someone else's) we're less likely to buy into the persuasive message. Thus, persuasive speech should appeal to one's own experience where appropriate and should resonate with the personal experience of the audience if possible.

Logos

Logos refers to the use of logic to persuade an audience and stands in direct opposition to "common sense." Though usually defined as "good judgment," common sense is actually nothing more than a combination of hearsay (unsubstantiated information) and popular opinion, and is used primarily for reasons related to political ideology. For example, "It's common sense that we need to lower taxes right now!" or "We need a 'common sense' approach to immigration reform!" Whereas common sense implies that no further explanation is necessary, logic demands a formal description of the thought process employed to come to specific conclusions. In other words, *logic* is a system of reasoning based on the internally consistent application of rules. The most fundamental distinction in logic between types of reasoning is between induction and deduction.

Inductive Logic

When we come to a general rule of understanding based on a collection of specific instances, we are using inductive logic. A classic illustration of inductive logic is the conclusion that all swans are white. This conclusion would likely be arrived at by someone who has only seen white swans and has never seen a black swan. Of course, black swans do exist, so this example also reveals that inductive logic is imperfect when it does not account for every possible instance that the conclusion extends to. This is an inherent risk of inductive reasoning. Whether based on general experience or scientific research, all reasoning that makes generalizations from a set of cases can yield only probable conclusions, not certain conclusions.

Deductive Logic

When we apply general rules (called premises) to specific instances, we are using deductive logic. The principles of deductive logic are demonstrated in the structure of the *syllogism* (a logical statement where a conclusion is drawn based on two premises that share a common term). Aristotle expresses a classic syllogism in the following figure:

Premise 1: Socrates is a man.

Premise 2: All men are mortal.

Conclusion: Therefore, Socrates is mortal.

In this case, the common term is "man," and because Socrates belongs to the category "man," any attribute that all men possess, Socrates must also possess by virtue of his belonging to that category. More formally written, the syllogism looks like this A (Socrates) = B (man), B (man) = C (mortal), therefore: A (Socrates) = C (mortal), where '=' is not interpreted as 'equals' but as 'is a member of the set'.

When the relationship between the premises and the conclusion cannot be supported, the result is a logical fallacy. Fallacies are incredibly common, but they represent the worst side of persuasion. Fallacies are tricks and disguises to fool an audience, not strong persuasive efforts. Unfortunately, unethical speakers frequently use fallacies, and audiences all too often fall for them.

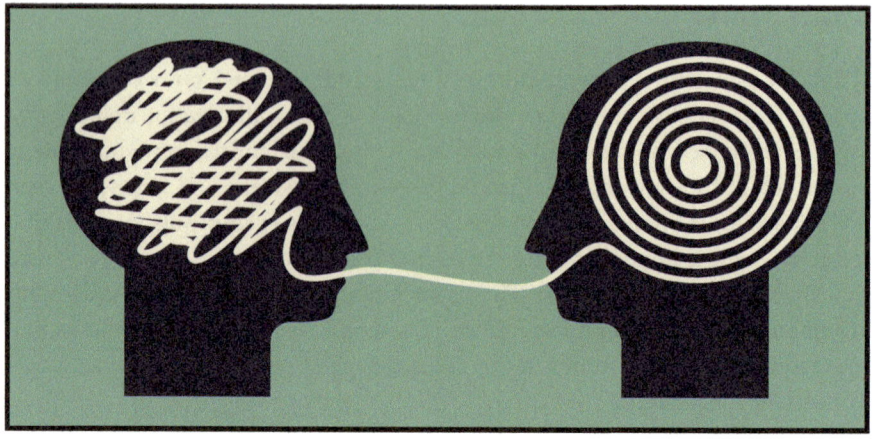

AD HOMINEM: This fallacy occurs when an author attacks his opponent instead of his opponent's argument.

Example: John claims that fossil fuels are affecting the climate but John has been married three times so we shouldn't believe what he says.

Example: A speaker in a debate states that his opponent has been at fault in two car accidents. The speaker cites this fact as evidence that his opponent's argument is not credible, even though this fact about his opponent's personal history is irrelevant to her argument.

AD POPULUM: This is an attempt to prove an argument as truthful simply because a large number of people believe it to be so.

Example: 90% of people eat meat. Therefore, being a vegetarian is unhealthy.

Example: A speaker references a study in which the majority of people in the world said they believed in God and life after death and claims it can, therefore, be assumed that there is definitely something waiting for the departed on the other side.

APPEAL TO AUTHORITY: In this fallacy, the author bases the validity of his argument on the premise that the argument is supported by someone famous or powerful.

Example: "If Kabbalah works for Madonna, then Kabbalah will work for you."

Example: The speaker refers the audience to Leonardo Da Vinci and George Bernard Shaw as famous vegetarians to prove the point that vegetarianism, by being embraced by such great minds, is the best dietary choice for everyone.

APPEAL TO EMOTION: A popular tactic among demagogues and dictators, this fallacy manipulates the emotional states of an audience to support an argument.

Example: Donald Trump incites a crowd to chant, "Lock her up!" at a campaign rally.

BEGGING THE QUESTION: This occurs when the premise of an argument contains (or assumes) its conclusion. Presuming the conclusion of an argument in one of its premises constitutes circular reasoning.

Example: Gracie: Gentlemen prefer blondes.

George: How do you know that?

Gracie: A gentleman told me so.

George: How did you know he was a gentleman?

Gracie: Because he preferred blondes.

(George Burns and Gracie Allen, quoted by Ronald J. Waicukauski et al. in "The Winning Argument." American Bar Association, 2001)

FALSE DICHOTOMY/FALSE DILEMMA: A fallacy that relies on the assumption that only two possible solutions exist, so that disproving one solution means the other solution appears to be the only logical conclusion.

Example: "I thought you were nice, but you then you didn't send me a Christmas card." (The underlying argument is that either one is both nice and a Christmas card sender, or if one is not a Christmas card sender, then one is not nice.)

Example: A speaker relates to the audience that as of yet no evidence of other intelligent life has been found in our galaxy. They go on to make the claim that we are all alone in the universe. (The underlying argument is that either we have found other intelligent life in our galaxy, or we are alone in the universe.)

HASTY GENERALIZATION: When the proponent uses too little evidence to support a sweeping generalization.

Example: Jeff and Lucy couldn't find any cool comics at the comic book store, so the comic book store doesn't have any cool comics.

Example: "I met two people from Philadelphia and they were loud and pushy. Obviously, Philadelphians are loud and pushy."

POST HOC/FALSE CAUSE: This fallacy confuses correlation and causation, that is, if one event precedes another event, it is concluded that it must also be the cause of that event. However, it is false that correlation in time always indicates a causal relation.

Example: "Since I've come to town there has been nothing but sunshine. You're welcome."

MISSING THE POINT: This fallacy occurs when the premise of an argument validly supports the conclusion, but the conclusion is not the one drawn by the author to which this argument is responding.

Example: Texting while driving is dangerous, so clearly cell phone companies should be held accountable when car accidents happen.

STRAW MAN: The author brings up one of his opponent's weaker, less central arguments and tears it apart, while pretending that this argument is the heart of the issue.

Example: My opponent argues for higher taxes on the wealthiest one percent. But I reject communism in all its forms.

RED HERRING: This is an attempt to distract the audience by straying from the topic at hand through introducing a separate argument the speaker feels is easier to speak to.

Example: Mother: Eat your peas, Bill.

Bill: Mommy, is there life on Mars?

Mother: I don't know, honey. Now eat your peas.

Bill: But mommy, did Martians build the pyramids?

Example: A lawyer who is supposed to be defending a client accused of money laundering makes the argument through testimonials and/or examples that the defendant can't be guilty because of the great things they've done for the community.

SLIPPERY SLOPE (the edge of the wedge, camel's nose) – This fallacy is the assertion that a relatively small first step will inevitably lead to a chain reaction of subsequent events culminating in some significant and disastrous impact/event that would inevitably occur, hence the very first step should not occur.

Example: First you enter your name, email address, and cell-phone number. Then before you know it, Big-Brother owns your soul.

Example: If we don't build a wall, more immigrants will come in, committing crimes, stealing and murdering until our entire way of life is destroyed.

ALTERNATIVE TRUTH: A fallacy made famous in the contemporary postmodern world that denies the reliability of given facts or truths. Journalist Leslie Grass writes of alternative truth: "The ideal subject of totalitarian rule is not the convinced Nazi or the dedicated communist, but people for whom the distinction between fact and fiction, true and false, no longer exists." (Leslie Grass 2017)

THE APPEAL TO CLOSURE: This fallacy makes the case that an argument, viewpoint, or conclusion must be accepted as final no matter how dubious it is or else the issue will remain unresolved, which is inconceivable since those involved would be denied "closure".

Example: "Though justice would be served if we sentenced you to life without parole, we need to execute you to provide closure to the case."

Example: "Even though it's not completely clear whether he committed the crime we should convict Mr. X so that the victim's family can get on with their life."

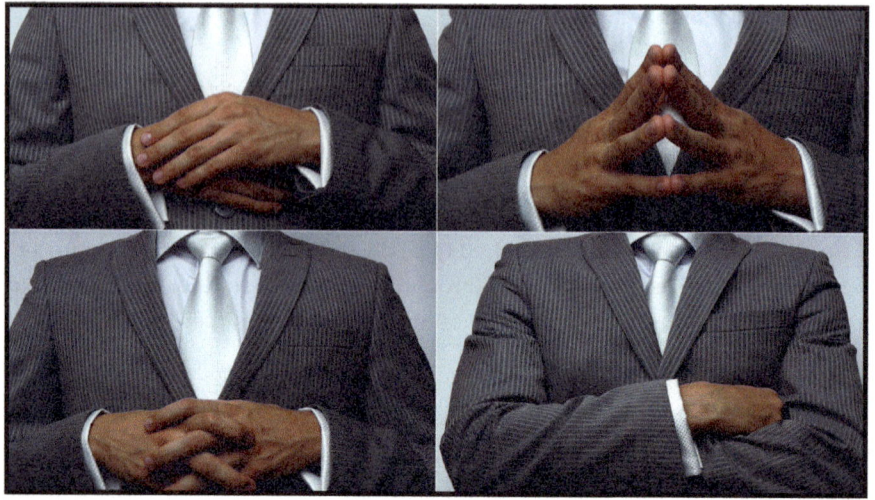

THE APPEAL TO HEAVEN: This deluded ethical argument stems from a claim of knowing the mind of God or a higher power.

> Example: One example of this fallacy is the concept of Manifest Destiny, where one group of people takes away the land of another because they claim that scripture or the word of God has given them the right to do so.

> Example: A speaker opposes the view that climate change is threatening life on earth using evidence from the Bible to the contrary and claiming that God will not allow harm to come to his creation.

Pathos

Pathos refers to the use of, or appeal to, emotions in persuasion. Even when logic, reasoning, evidence, and research are lacking, audiences may be moved by a speaker's passion. A **demagogue,** for example, is a speaker who makes use of emotion, prejudice, and fear to persuade an audience. To some extent, pathos is also dependent upon ethos. For an audience to be persuaded by a speaker's emotional manipulation, they must, on some level, trust in the character of that speaker.

How are emotions manipulated through speech? Topic choice, verbal cues, nonverbal cues, and show stopping can all play a role in the manipulation of emotion in a speech.

Topic Choice

Some topics lend themselves particularly well to emotional manipulation, while others do not. For example, the time-worn debate over abortion is so predisposed to emotional appeals that even when speakers attempt to approach it objectively the results are often clouded by pathos. Other topics like *recycling* are relatively less controversial on the surface, but can lend themselves to the use of emotion in the right context. Generally speaking, when you approach your topic from the perspective of *values* (deeply held personal commitments about right and wrong), pathos has a much greater chance of coming into play. *Attitudes* (liking or disliking) and *beliefs* (truth or falsehood) tend to generate less volatile reactions when challenged, though they can still provoke strong emotions to the extent that they support value systems.

Verbal Cues

We have a visceral reaction to some words based on their repeated use in prior contexts; therefore, it's possible to touch on an audience's emotions simply through the use of language. Consider the differences between words like "ecstatic" vs. "glad" to describe happiness, "dejected" vs. "glum" to describe sadness, "terrified" vs. "anxious" to describe fear, and "tortured" vs. "hurt" to describe pain. In each of these pairs, the first word has more emotional impact than the second. However, sometimes language is used in an attempt to reduce the emotional impact of ideas. Former President George W. Bush and officials in his administration infamously substituted the words "enhanced interrogation" for "torture" to lessen the emotional response to policies on the handling of those held on suspicion of terrorism. Strategic ambiguity, using less specific language to hide or omit information, is another form of doublespeak. A teenager responding with "Not much, just hung out with friends" to a parental inquiry of "What did you do today?" could be engaging in strategic ambiguity if the real answer is "I flunked a test, dented the car, and spent five hours playing video games in somebody's basement."

Nonverbal Cues

Delivery is a holistic concept and therefore all aspects of nonverbal communication play a role in emotional persuasion, but there are still several key features that stand out: facial expressions, eye contact, and paralanguage.

- **FACIAL EXPRESSIONS:** Beneath the skin of our face, a layer of delicate interconnected muscles convey happiness, sadness, pain, anxiety, anger, surprise, and a host of other more subtle emotions. Even when we don't want to show our emotions, they often betray us through facial expressions. In psychology, "emotional contagion theory" even suggests that looking at a face with a particular emotion on display transmits that emotion to the viewer. In other words, looking at happy faces makes us happy and looking at sad faces makes us sad.

- **EYE CONTACT:** Looking at audiences directly and (in most cases) providing sustained, individualized eye contact is vital to emotional persuasion. As noted above, pathos is somewhat dependent upon ethos, and we tend not to trust other people and their emotional appeals when they don't look at us in the eyes.

- **PARALANGUAGE:** Paralanguage is the component of voice communication contributed by intonation, pitch and speed of speaking, hesitation noises and volume. In addition to being your primary means of communication in public speech, the voice is also a very sensitive conductor of emotion. Every subtlety of our present emotional state is broadcast through the voice. Absence of emotion in the voice is referred to as being monotone and that is to be avoided. The emotional tone of your voice should mirror the content of your speech and remain consistent throughout. For example, tragedy should be treated with a somber tone.

Nonverbal Consistency Theory intuitively suggests that trust and credibility will be vastly diminished if nonverbal cues don't match the verbal message. For example, smiling and having an upbeat tone of voice when reporting bad news would be greeted with obvious skepticism.

Show Stopping

Sometimes pathos is used illogically to force a perspective on an audience or to silence other speakers. Imagine that two people are discussing drug policy in the United States. A participant in a debate thinks marijuana should be legalized for public sale and consumption. Another participant in the debate, disagrees, but (instead of addressing the issue directly) talks about how her grandmother recently died. Because her grandmother hated all illegal drugs, it's a terrible idea to legalize marijuana. Furthermore, Person B thinks that anyone who argues against her is disrespecting the memory of her grandmother.

This is a patently fallacious argument, but surprisingly effective depending on the circumstances and the audience.

Types of Persuasive Speech

Persuasive speeches can be molded into several different forms based upon the nature of the persuasive claim (the "type" of persuasive speech) and the method of organization. As with informative speeches, persuasive speeches come in a variety of different types, but based on a proposition rather than a lesson. These include:

1. Proposition of Fact
A statement asserting something about some aspect of reality.

The following is an example of a Proposition of Fact.

Specific Purpose Statement: To persuade my audience that some form of human consciousness persists after death.

Central Idea: Spiritual life persists after the death of the organic body because people have had encounters with the afterlife such as seeing the light and meeting their loved ones who passed away.

2. Proposition of Policy
A statement urging or recommending collective action or a change in collective action through official channels.

The following is an example of a Proposition of Policy.

Specific Purpose Statement: To persuade my audience that people aged 18-65 should be required to work in order to receive public assistance.

Central Idea: Problems arise when recipients of public assistance don't work and the solution is to require them to work to be eligible for these benefits.

3. Proposition of Value

This is an ethical statement about right vs. wrong or good vs. bad (e.g. "Diversity is not universally good.").

The following is an example of a Proposition of Value.

Specific Purpose Statement: To persuade my audience that courage is a worthy value to have and that it should be exercised every day.

Central Idea: Courage is important every day of your life.

Methods of Organization

All the methods for organizing a speech covered under informative speaking are applicable here as well. In addition, however, there are some valuable strategies for ordering main points that apply directly to persuasive speaking. These include:

1. Recency: The main points of the speech are organized so that the best arguments and evidence come last. This leaves the audience with the strongest possible impression of your persuasive message.

2. Primacy: The opposite of recency. Main points of the speech are organized so that the best arguments and evidence are presented up front. This is especially useful with skeptical or hostile audiences. Initially impressive arguments may capture their attention and give you a chance to make your case.

3. Problem/Solution: This strategy divides the body of the speech into main points based on problem and solution. In some cases, multiple problems and solutions are presented and, through the process of elimination, the proposal offered by the speaker is ultimately recommended.

4. Monroe's Motivated Sequence: This strategy is a variation of problem/solution. The audience is offered a "need" (a problem that needs solving), a "satisfaction" (a solution to the problem), "visualization" scenarios where the problem is solved and/or not solved, and "action" where the audience is called upon to do something to enact the satisfaction/solution.

Referring back to the organizational strategies offered for the informative speech, you may notice that *reorganization* (deliberately choosing the order of your events or main points) plays an important role in persuasion. Main points must be ordered according to the *principle of complexity* (simpler information is presented before more complex information), but can be further organized to achieve a recency or primacy effect, a problem/solution strategy, or to enact Monroe's Motivated Sequence.

6

Commemorative Speaking

Thomas S. Wright, PhD *Temple University*

Maxine Gesualdi *West Chester University*

Commemorative Speeches: An Overview

Previous chapters focused on the skills you need to succeed as a citizen and in your professional life. In this chapter, we focus on commemorative speeches. One of the most common speech types, commemorative speeches celebrate special events in a person's life. Commemorative speeches are so common that Aristotle in *On Rhetoric* devotes an entire section to what the Greek's called *epideictic* speeches. An epideictic speech either praises a person for virtuous actions or blames them for bad deeds. While we see fewer speeches of blame today than in Ancient Greece, the importance of the epideictic or ceremonial speech of praise has changed little over the past 2,400 years. Our modern lives are punctuated with special celebrations and events that provide opportunities for you to "say a few words." For example, you may have given an acceptance speech to an organization that gave you a scholarship. Or perhaps you gave a toast at your brother's wedding. In the future, you may be asked to present an award to honor a co-worker or a community leader. In each of these situations, you use your public speaking skills to celebrate an event, a person, or a group.

The purpose of a commemorative speech is to **express the importance of the moment and the people involved.** It is given to publicly celebrate or commemorate a special *occasion*. A special occasion is a time set apart from everyday life and its events to reflect on and publicly state what we value most. Since the time of the Greeks, commemorative speeches have had a ritualistic quality, which means they elevate and transcend our everyday lives but in a way that is familiar. In other words, social and cultural expectations often determine how you should perform commemorative speeches. What does an audience expect when they hear a eulogy? A eulogy is a speech given in praise or memory of someone, usually someone who is deceased. Based on cultural expectations, a eulogy must express sadness at the loss of a loved one and joyfully celebrate her or his life. What should you do when you accept an award? A speech of acceptance must include a thank you to the organization or person who presented the award. What do wedding guests think is an appropriate story in a toast? A toast should be cheerful and reflect on the special nature of the occasion. In this sense, all of these speeches are ritualistic. Each type of commemorative speech reflects a set of cultural values governed by a set of situational requirements. In the following sections, we will walk you through the process of applying your existing public speaking skills to the process of constructing several types of commemorative speeches.

In this chapter, you will learn:

- How to apply the public speaking skills you already learned to commemorative speaking.

- The preliminary rules for preparing a commemorative speech.

- Detailed insights and advice for constructing six common types of commemorative speeches:

  - Toast

  - Speech of Introduction

  - Speech of Presentation

  - Speech of Acceptance

  - Speech of Commemoration

  - Eulogy

Commemorative Speeches: Skills Application, Audience Analysis, and Reducing Apprehension

Public Speaking Skills Application

Preparing a commemorative speech will involve the same public speaking skills you have learned up to this point, but you will apply them for a different purpose. An effective commemorative speech requires that you use an organizational pattern that fits your personal style, helps the audience follow the flow of the presentation, and meets the criteria for the specific type of commemorative presentation. For example, the chronological organizational pattern used for many informative speeches is used often for speeches of introduction and eulogies. However, many times commemorative speeches use creative organizational patterns and themes.

An effective commemorative speech requires you to use many of the same delivery techniques and skills that you use in informative and persuasive speaking. The delivery skills of maintaining eye contact, using other nonverbal forms of communication, speaking clearly at an appropriate volume, using dynamic vocal range, and avoiding distracting gestures or movements are also important in commemorative speeches. In addition, you will use the same modes of presentation. Most commemorative speeches use the extemporaneous mode of presentation. One key difference you will find is that commemorative speeches

are often less formal or more conversational than informative or persuasive professional presentations. For example, when speaking to introduce someone to an audience, you may be upbeat and speak with greater range because your purpose is to enliven the crowd and raise their expectations for the featured guest.

Finally, the process for selecting content for a commemorative speech is not so different from your preparation for an informative or persuasive speech. In each case, your goal is to find the most accurate sources and use them effectively. For a commemorative presentation, as discussed later in the chapter, you must include accurate details and up-to-date information. However, while it is important to note who said a famous quote or authored the piece of poetry or literature you included, no one expects you to cite the source of personal information included in the speech.

When considering the purpose of your commemorative speech, our advice is:

- Apply the organization and content selection skills discussed in previous chapters.

- Review the criteria for each type of commemorative speech discussed later in this chapter.

- Determine whether your speech will be memorized, extemporaneous, or scripted.

A Distinct Audience

The audience for a commemorative speech is different from those at an informative or persuasive presentation. Specifically, the audience for a commemorative speech connects more intimately to the content of the speech than an audience for an informational or persuasive presentation. Toasts and eulogies are the perfect examples of this difference. A toast, as you will learn, is not for a generic audience. Its purpose is to celebrate a person or event that connects directly to that specific audience at that exact time. When you are called on to deliver a toast at your best friend's wedding, the audience is there to celebrate that specific couple in a very personal way. In contrast, consider how the toast at your friend's wedding is different from a speech to the city council about adding bike lanes. While the citizens at the council meeting have an interest in the topic, their connection to it is on a much less personal level.

When considering the audience for your commemorative speech, our advice is:

- Find out as much as you can about the audience using techniques you learned in the previous chapter on audience analysis. Knowing who may attend will affect content selection and delivery.

- Think of yourself as a surrogate or representative for the audience. For example, not everyone will make a toast, so you are speaking for everyone in attendance.

- Consider the emotional needs of the audience. How do you want them to feel and what content and language selections can you make to reflect that feeling?

Reducing Apprehension

You also need to practice the techniques you learned for managing public speaking apprehension. Almost everyone feels nervous in public speaking situations. Whichever term you choose to apply, apprehension, "stage fright," or "nervousness," nonetheless, the heightened energy of your apprehensive state shows that you care about the situation and the audience. It is natural to want to perform well and meet the needs of the audience. What makes you different is that you have learned a set of techniques for managing your apprehension and those are just as important when giving a commemorative speech as they are when presenting in class or at work. The setting, purpose, and time requirements for commemorative speeches also influence any apprehension you feel about your speech.

The settings for commemorative speeches are often less formal than those in professional presentations. For example, you can treat a speech of introduction for a new manager to the office or a guest pastor at church less formally and in a more relaxed way than a report over annual sales or a proposal to build a new adult care facility in town. As we discussed, the purpose of a commemorative speech is to mark a special occasion that reflects how you feel about the person or event. Because the purpose of the speech is less formal and more about creating connections and positive feelings, you should approach the situation as one in which the expectations for your performance are different.

Unlike a work presentation, the purpose of a commemorative speech is not to demonstrate your mastery of the topic. Instead, in a commemorative speech you want to connect with an audience that is already prepared to embrace you with feelings of good will. The purpose of the ceremony, of that moment in time, is tied to the emotions of the audience. The audience wants you to succeed. Remember, you are their surrogate. You represent them. They are not there to find fault but to support you. Finally, you will see later in the chapter that the time expectations for a commemorative speech are generally much shorter than a traditional informative or persuasive presentation. The relatively short time you have to speak may lessen any apprehension you experience. For example, a speech of introduction is usually only two to three minutes.

When managing your public speaking apprehension, our advice is:

- Practice the techniques for reducing public speaking apprehension.

- To reduce your apprehension and prepare yourself for the occasion, find out as much as you can about the setting. For example: When will you speak in the ceremony's agenda? Will you have a microphone? Will you be on a dais? Will there be a podium to hold notes? Knowing these details will help you prepare and be confident in your delivery.

Rules for Preparing a Commemorative Speech

While every type of commemorative speech has its own requirements, there are standard rules you should follow in preparing your presentation. These rules include keeping your speech brief, doing your research, using specific details, using pathos or making an emotional connection, and making figurative language choices.

Rule 1: Keep Your Speech Brief

Commemorative speeches are brief and reflect their specific purpose or event. Remember, commemorative speeches are often included as a part of a large and elaborate ceremony that may include a number of speakers, officials, dignitaries, executives, religious figures, or honorees. It is more important to leave a lasting impression with the audience through brevity and vivid language rather than thoroughness. Because you are the surrogate for the audience, you should keep in mind that your speech is not why they are attending the event. Therefore, your brevity will help the ceremony or event progress smoothly. You must practice your speech with a timer to ensure that you keep the speech short.

When timing your speech, our advice is:

- Find out from the event organizers how long they would like you to speak.

- Practice for time a few times to ensure you are staying within time limits.

- Respect the audience, the occasion, and the other speakers by using your allotted time and no more.

Rule 2: Do Your Research

Informative and persuasive speeches require extensive research. You use books, newspaper articles, websites, government documents, and interviews to provide credible information or to create persuasive appeals. Commemorative speeches do not require as much research. However, a good commemorative speech will need specific information that will personalize the speech and accurately reflect the event and people you are honoring. As the speaker, you are responsible for giving the audience accurate and timely information.

When conducting your research, our advice is:

- If your speech is about a person (introduction or eulogy), check all available web resources and talk to people who know the person being celebrated. You may include anecdotes or stories from friends, colleagues, and loved ones.

- If your speech involves a specific event or award, find out the purpose and history of the event/award.

- Ask the event sponsors who will be attending the event and how many people they expect to attend. You do not want to be surprised by your audience size.

- Talk to previous presenters. Do they have any useful tips or advice?

- Look for sample speeches or examples. There are many excellent examples available on youtube.com or via a simple Google search. These examples will help you set the tone for your speech and better understand the type of information you need to include.

Rule 3: Fact Check Your Details

Although commemorative speeches require less research than informative or persuasive speeches, the research you conduct for commemorative speeches should focus on detailed pieces of information that demonstrate your understanding of the person, event, or award. Using detailed, factual information also helps you meet your responsibility as a knowledgeable and conscientious speaker.

When fact checking the content for your speech, our advice is:

- Double-check the accuracy of all of your facts, quotes, readings, and anecdote/stories. If you are speaking to an organization, giving a speech of introduction, or commemorating an event, be sure to check with the event organizers if you are unsure of any details.

- Double-check the names of everyone mentioned in your speech for both accuracy and pronunciation.

- Double-check the titles used in the organization (President, CFO) or in the family (uncle or second cousin, grandmother or grandma).

- Ensure all chronological and biographical information is correct.

- Practice your speech so that you are familiar with the quotes, dates, and names you will be using.

Rule 4: Create Emotional Connections and Express Shared Values

Commemorative speeches evoke a broader range of emotions than informative and persuasive speeches. They will sometimes mix humor and sadness, joy and sorrow, pride and happiness. While informative speeches rarely include emotional language, the purpose of some commemorative speeches is to create an emotional response for its own sake. Eulogies are the clearest example of the emotional focus and range of commemorative speeches. Other commemorative speeches including a toast or speech of acceptance demonstrate the emotional connection every speaker hopes to achieve. For example, when you give a toast, you are making a public proclamation of joy. In a speech of acceptance, you would be providing a public "thank you" to the organization or person who bestowed the award on you.

In addition, creating an emotional connection exemplifies the special role that audiences play in commemorative speeches. The communication theorist Kenneth Burke developed the concept of identification, which referred to the act of creating a sense of commonality or connection between an audience and a speaker or between members of an audience. While Burke uses the term generally to mean any persuasive act that creates a sense of connection, we can see that creating a feeling of identification is one of the central purposes of commemorative speaking. Commemorative speeches, like those given in the

U.S. on the 4th of July to honor the founding of the United States, lean heavily on the use of identification around patriotism and American ideals to generate a sense of togetherness among all members of the audience.

To bring emotional focus to your speech, our advice is:

- Consider the purpose of your speech. Some commemorative speeches (introduction, presentation, acceptance) are about shared values while other types (eulogies, commemorative) are about the public expression of private emotions. We will review each of these speech types later in the chapter.

- Before outlining and writing your speech, reflect on and write out one or two specific emotions or values you want your speech to evoke.

- When you write or outline your speech, note which emotion(s) or values you want each section of your speech to create. This will bring focus to your speech and delivery.

- Before writing and practicing your speech, reflect on how you feel and what you believe the audience feels or values. As a surrogate for the audience, you are responsible for representing how they feel or what they value.

- In order to build toward the emotional release you have planned, determine the best content to expresses these emotions (such as anecdotes, quotes, or visual aids) and which organizational pattern (topical, chronological, cause-effect, or creative pattern you develop) will build toward an emotional release.

- If your speech is on a particularly emotional topic or situation, consider how to best control your own emotions when you are practicing your delivery.

- Consider how you can create a sense of identification. Why are all the audience members at the event? What values, beliefs, or attitudes do they all share? What are some key things that everyone would agree on?

- Search for sample speeches or examples. There are many excellent examples available on youtube.com or via a simple Google search. These examples will help you set the tone for your speech and better understand the type of information you need to include.

Rule 5: Use Figurative Language

One of the unique and exciting characteristics of commemorative speeches is that you can use more figurative language in your delivery than in informative or persuasive speeches. Figurative language is language that moves beyond the literal meanings of words or phrases found in the dictionary. Figurative language is more poetic, embellished, visual, emotive, and exaggerated than everyday language. Think of this when considering the use of language: commemorative speeches do not happen every day so they should not use everyday language. The language should paint a picture in the audience members' minds to help them see what you are saying. Because the purpose of commemorative speeches is to evoke an emotional response or create a sense of identification, your choice of words or phrases should reflect that purpose. Unlike the straightforward language used in an informative speech, the words and phrases in a commemorative speech serve a different purpose. For example, if you were to eulogize your grandma, you would not describe her cookies as just "good" would you? You might use a metaphor, or a comparison using two unlike concepts, and call them "heavenly"! You might use hyperbole, or exaggeration, and say, "grandma's cookies were the best cookies in the world!" It is easy to see how using figurative language relates closely to rule #4, creating an emotional connection. Remember, commemorative speeches aspire to create a strong connection to the audience and painting a picture helps reach this goal.

When selecting the figurative language for your speech, our advice is:

- Use metaphors, similes, hyperbole, alliteration, repetition, and imagery or sensory details.

- Use a thesaurus. While you never want to rely too much on a thesaurus or choose words you are not comfortable saying, finding just the right word or phrase to express how you feel is worth a few extra minutes.

- Use resources to find inspirational or famous quotes, poems, or religious verses. A well-chosen quote or religious verse can express how you feel and create identification for the audience.

- Consider using song lyrics. Depending on the type of speech you are giving, lyrics are an easy way to enliven your speech, reflect an emotion you are trying to evoke, and create a sense of identification.

- Avoid clichés or overused phrases. If it does not express exactly how you feel or seems like it is said in everyday conversation, look for a different word or phrase.

Figure 6.1 **Rules for Preparing a Commemorative Speech**

Keep Your Speech Brief

Do Your Research

Check Your Facts

Create Emotional Connection and Express Shared Values

Use Figurative Language

Common Types of Commemorative Speeches

The Toast

A toast is a short commemorative speech that celebrates a person or group and is a custom in Western cultures. During a toast, the speaker holds a filled drinking glass. At the end of the speech, the speaker ritualistically raises her or his glass into the air as a gesture of good will and asks the audience members to raise their glasses as well. Then, everyone takes a drink. Toasts are often common at events that celebrate family milestones (an engagement, wedding, or anniversary party) or mark achievements in organizations (retirement, award ceremonies, or reunions).

Delivery Tips

- Keep your toast brief. A toast is rarely more than one to three minutes (200-300 words). There are often more than one or two people giving a toast.

- Get everyone's attention before you begin. Your goal is to honor those being toasted and bring an emotional focus to the event.

- Encourage everyone in the audience to be prepared to toast. Everyone should have a glass and be prepared to raise it as a symbolic gesture.

- Keep your remarks informal and relaxed to match the tone and expectations of a celebration.

Organization Suggestions

- A toast usually follows a simple organizational pattern:

    - welcome the guests and thank them for attending,

    - acknowledge those responsible for the event (parents, organization),

    - state who or what you are toasting,

    - state your relationship to person(s) or the event,

    - provide detail to personalize the toast and make an emotional connection to the person being toasted and to the audience (an anecdote, example, quote, religious reading/quote),

    - add a look toward the future (e.g. "many years to come"),

    - and end with a thank you. You should add a reminder to the audience to raise their glasses at the end of your toast.

Content Guidelines

- Do research to make sure that you know all the names you need to mention and how to pronounce them.

- Toasts often include humorous quotes or anecdotes about the person(s) being toasted or the event. Be sure that your humor is in "good taste" and does not involve inside jokes that many in the audience will not understand.

- Toasts should make it clear why the person(s) or the event is special. What makes this event toast-worthy?

- The tone of a toast should almost always be positive and optimistic. You are either wishing someone good luck for the future (wedding, retirement) or reflecting on the importance of an event and what it means to the audience (holiday celebration, work event).

- A toast is not a roast. While humor is often used when giving a toast, your goal is not to embarrass, make fun of, or humiliate anyone in attendance. Save any questionable or potentially embarrassing stories for another time.

Speech of Introduction

A speech of introduction is a general term used to refer to any speech that is announcing or previewing another speaker or event. It is given in preparation for something more to come. There are a wide variety of speeches of introduction including welcoming a new employee and introducing a keynote speaker or a special guest at an event.

Delivery Tips

- A speech of introduction should be two to three minutes long (300-400 words). Because your remarks are preparing the audience for a longer speech, you should keep them brief.

- An important goal for the speech of introduction is to focus the audience's attention. It is your responsibility to use your delivery to engage the audience and hold their attention. You want to shift their attention from interaction to listening.

- The speaking style for a speech of introduction should be professional. Because speeches of introduction are used most often in a professional or organizational setting, you should be prepared, make consistent eye contact, and speak with authority.

Organization Suggestions

- A speech of introduction follows a standard organizational pattern:

    - thank everyone for attending or welcome the audience to the event,

    - remind them of the purpose of the event,

    - provide information about the next speaker or agenda item of the event,

    - build anticipation,

    - and welcome the speaker (with applause) or kick off the event.

Content Guidelines

- Do your research and double-check that all of the information you have about the speaker or event is correct. It is a best practice to review your information with the person you are introducing and the event coordinators. Oftentimes, a speaker will give you a biography of information you can include.

- State the purpose or relevance of the event. Why is the audience in attendance? Why is the speaker in attendance? What will the audience learn or take away from attending?

- Briefly thank those who organized or sponsored the event.

- Establish the credibility and credentials of the speaker. You may include any of the following types of professionally appropriate information: degree(s) or certifications, schools attended, experience, previous awards, prior presentations, grants received, and title(s).

- Depending on the event, you may be asked to include basic pertinent personal information. You do not have to provide a complete biography but sometimes you may include a speaker's hometown, hobbies, family status, and travel experiences. The person you are introducing and/or the event coordinator can help you determine if personal information should be included for the purpose of the event.

- One way to build anticipation is to preview the speaker's topic with a teaser. You are not responsible for providing a summary but offering a glimpse of what the audience will be hearing may motivate them to pay better attention. This can also be done as an attention getter.

Speech of Presentation

A speech of presentation occurs when a speaker gives an award, honor, or commendation to a recipient or organization. Similar to the speech of introduction, this type of speech leads into the main focus of the occasion. You may be asked to announce the winner of a scholarship, a local leader who is receiving an award for public service, or a sports league commissioner presenting a trophy to the local girls' softball team. In each case, your responsibilities are like those for the speech of introduction. You need to highlight the accomplishment of the recipient.

Delivery Tips

- A speech of presentation should be one to two minutes long (200-300 words). Your remarks prepare the audience to celebrate achievement so keep them brief.

- Do research to make sure that you know all the names you need to mention and how to pronounce them.

- An important goal for the speech of presentation is to focus the audience's attention. You want to shift their attention from interaction to listening.

- The speaking style for a speech of presentation should be enthusiastic but respectful. You should be prepared, make consistent eye contact, and use open and engaging language while speaking with passion.

Organization Suggestions

- A speech of presentation follows a simple organizational pattern:

    - thank everyone for attending or welcome them to the event,

    - provide background information or context for the award, honor, or commendation,

    - briefly thank everyone who participated in the process or who were nominated,

    - and reveal the name of the person or organization.

Content Guidelines

- Do your research and double-check that all of the information you have about the award and the person or organization receiving it is correct. It is a best practice to review your information with the event coordinators.

- Briefly, explain the purpose of the award, honor, or commendation. You may include a brief history, who sponsors it and why, the ideals it represents, or the criteria used during the selection process. While there is no perfect combination of information, your goal is to provide context for the audience so they can appreciate the importance of the award.

- Depending on the award, you may need to explain why the person or organization was chosen as the recipient.

- Depending on the award, you may also convey what the award means to you as a person, as a member of the community, or as a representative of an organization.

Speech of Acceptance

A speech of acceptance is a short speech you would give when receiving an award, honor, or commendation. You might be asked to say a few words after receiving an award for yourself or as a representative of an organization. An important characteristic of a speech of acceptance is that while you are receiving recognition, the purpose of the award is to link to a larger social good or shared value. For example, a scholarship from a local club is not just about awarding money to you but is also about publicly recognizing the importance of hard work and the value of higher education.

Delivery Tips

- A speech of acceptance is rarely more than one to two minutes (100-200 words). There is often more than one person accepting an award or there may be multiple awards given out, so you do not want to dominate the proceedings.

- Your delivery should demonstrate humility and enthusiasm for being chosen. It is important to use open and engaging body language, vocal range and variety, and make consistent eye contact. You need to show the audience that you are thankful and worthy of the award.

- Whether or not you know in advance that you will be receiving the award, be prepared to accept it. Even outlining a few remarks will make you less nervous and will help you avoid veering off the subject and taking too much time.

Organization Suggestions

- A speech of acceptance follows a standard organizational pattern:

  – thank the presenter and the organization or person who bestowed the award,

  – give credit or recognize other people or organizations that could have received the award,

  – and briefly state what the award means to you.

Content Guidelines

- Thank those giving the award. Do your research so that you know who (person, organization) is giving the award and its significance. How long has it been awarded? Who else has received it? What values, beliefs, or ideals does it represent?

- Be prepared to state what the award means to you. If you are accepting a scholarship, you will want to state how it will help you meet your expenses (and have more time to study). If you are receiving a civic or organizational award, you will want to convey how you are connected to the community or organization.

- Briefly mention other people or organizations that could have also been given the award.

- Thank those who helped you on your path to accepting the award. This may include your parents, siblings, coach, co-workers, boss, etc.

Speech of Commemoration

A speech of commemoration honors, pays tribute to, or celebrates an event, place, or person. Three key characteristics of these speeches are that they take place in public ceremonies, represent widely held beliefs or values, and deal with something in the past. For example, a speech given before a 4th of July parade commemorates the founding of the United States and will mention widely held American values such as freedom, liberty, and unity. Speeches of commemoration are often given on historic anniversaries (e.g. December 7th) or holidays (e.g. Memorial Day) and to celebrate important people (e.g. Susan B. Anthony).

Delivery Tips

- A speech of commemoration may be either one to two minutes or five to six minutes, depending on the occasion and precedent. You should ask the organizers how long speeches have been in the past or how long they would like you to speak.

- Your delivery should be well-practiced, formal, and fit the tone or mood of the occasion. Some commemorative speeches are focused on memorializing a tragic event (e.g. 9/11), while others celebrate the life of an important public figure (e.g. Dr. Martin Luther King).

Organization Suggestions

- A speech of commemoration follows a standard organizational pattern:

  - thank everyone for attending or welcome them to the event,

  - thank the event organizers,

  - provide background information or context for the commemoration,

  - and discuss how the event or person is relevant today (this often includes the audience's shared values or beliefs). You may also discuss how the events of the past or the celebrated person's life relate to the future.

Content Guidelines

- Do your research and double-check that all of the information you have about the event or the person being commemorated is correct.

- Establish why the event or person is being celebrated. What about the event or the person elevates them to a place of honor?

- Provide specific details about the event or the person being commemorated. In this way, the speech of commemoration is similar to an informative speech. You cannot assume that everyone in attendance is familiar with the basic information about the event or the biographical details of the person you are celebrating.

- Use quotes or readings from significant individuals to highlight the importance of the event or person being celebrated.

- Perhaps more so than any other type of commemorative speech, a speech of commemoration uses stories or a narrative format. Because you are recounting a historical event or the life of a person, consider what details are necessary to construct the narrative of what happened or recount the important events of a person's life.

- Some commemorative events will be attended by those who were directly involved in the event or know the person being honored. It is important to mention their presence and allow the crowd to applaud.

- Provide image-rich examples that focus on values (courage, sacrifice, hard work).

Eulogy

A eulogy is a speech given to celebrate the life of a person who is now deceased. They are often given at a memorial service and the audience includes family members, friends, and co-workers. A eulogy must walk a complicated path between recognizing the emotional pain caused by the person's death and celebrating her or his life. This complicated path highlights how eulogies are distinct from the other types of commemorative speeches we have discussed. The content or purpose is more emotional than other types of speeches, and the speaker is allowed to be more emotional. Additionally, you are responsible for representing the feelings of the audience. Because not everyone in attendance will be asked to give a eulogy, the selected speakers should reflect the thoughts and feelings of the audience. Your goal is to get the audience to transcend their sorrow and see how fortunate they were to have known the deceased.

Delivery Tips

- Eulogies range in length but are usually three to five minutes long (300-500 words). It is common for there to be a number of speakers or religious figures scheduled to speak, so be sure to find out how much time you have to speak.

- Your delivery should be well practiced, formal, and fit the tone or mood of the occasion. As discussed above, it is important to recognize the solemnity of the occasion but also show the joy that a person brought to your life.

- One of the more challenging aspects of delivering a eulogy is managing your emotions. Practicing your speech will often help because you will be better prepared for emotional moments in your speech.

Organization Guidelines

- There are many excellent resources available for organizing a eulogy. You should not be embarrassed to use templates or premade organizational patterns. It is an emotional time, and anything that may help reduce your stress or anxiety is important.

- A common organizational pattern is to:
    - thank those in attendance,
    - state your relationship to the deceased (if it is not obvious or already known),
    - provide a brief biographical overview of the person's life,
    - mention those things in life that she or he loved most,
    - show how her or his life affected those in the audience,
    - and how the audience members can honor her or his passing.

- You can also use a thematic approach that centers on her or his life (biographical, chronological), accomplishments, roles they played (mother, wife, dancer), or personality characteristics.

Content Guidelines

- One of the more challenging aspects of giving a eulogy is managing the amount of content available with the amount of time you are allotted. Imagine the   challenge of summarizing a person's life and what she or he meant to you (and everyone in the audience) in just a few minutes.

- Acknowledge the loss to the family, friends, and colleagues but recognize how the deceased person's spirit will live on in everyday events and actions.

- Use quotes (either famous or from family members), a poem, song lyrics, or religious readings to bring focus to the person's life or to the impact the person had on the lives of those in attendance.

- Use anecdotes or stories to illustrate aspects of the person's life, personality, or important relationships.

- Recognize the person's uniqueness. How was she or he different or special? Be sure to use an example or anecdote to highlight this.

- Use your personal relationship to focus on the particular role the person played in life. For example, if you were the person's colleague, you should focus on that particular aspect of her or his life. You are representative of all of her or his work relationships.

- Ask friends, family, and colleagues what they will remember most about the deceased. Do they have a favorite anecdote? What are three words they would use to describe her or him? What is the funniest thing he or she ever said or did? This allows you to meet your goal of honoring the person's life, but it also allows you to include the audience.

Conclusion

The purpose of a commemorative speech is to express the importance of a milestone moment and the people involved. It is given to publicly celebrate or commemorate a special occasion. In your personal and professional life, you will at some point be asked to deliver a commemorative speech. In this chapter, we have provided you with advice, rules, and guideline for preparing for six distinct types of commemorative speeches: Toast, Speech of Introduction, Speech of Presentation, Speech of Acceptance, Speech of Commemoration, and Eulogy.

7

Introductions and Conclusions

Dr. Sandra French
Radford University

Introductions

The beginning of a speech is often the hardest to create. Have you ever heard the saying that it takes only 7 seconds to create a first impression? (Goman, 2011). Your introduction is your first impression. Use it to pique the interest of your listeners and establish common ground. Too often speakers give little time and attention to how they will begin a speech, opting instead for the strategy of simply stating, for example, "Hi, I'm Sandy, and today I'm going to talk to you about ways to reduce pollution." This type of introduction generates little enthusiasm on the part of listeners and fails to convey a speaker's genuine interest in sharing information with listeners. An effective introduction helps create a favorable first impression with listeners. It also boosts your confidence as a speaker, and generates interest in the speech.

What is an audience looking for in an introduction? Effective introductions include the following elements:

Figure 7.1

1. **Get the attention of the audience**

2. **Reveal the topic**

3. **Relate topic to the audience (WIIFM)**

4. **Establish credibility**

5. **Preview the Body of the Speech**

Step One: Getting the attention of your audience

There are several options that speakers have for getting their audience's attention. While specific options for introducing a speech are many, we will focus here on five general strategies to make an impact:

- Ask a question.

- Share a startling fact or statistic.

- Use a relevant quotation.

- Tell a humorous story or joke.

- Use a real or hypothetical illustration.

Ask a question. When a speaker begins with a question for the audience, the answer is usually an obvious one, but the question is asked in order to make a point to the audience. Let's say you are going to do an informative speech on cancer. A speaker might ask audience members to stand up if they know someone affected by cancer. This type of visual "answer" could help a speaker show the widespread impact of the disease and "set the stage" for the speech. However, a speaker must analyze the audience adequately so as to have confidence in the answer audience members will supply to the question. For example, during one public speaking class that I taught, a student wanted to convince his fellow classmates to ride the University-provided bus transportation around campus, rather than driving their cars, in an effort to help protect the environment. He conducted research about the percentage of students that drove to campus daily rather than using the bus system, and he felt well prepared to give his speech. However, he neglected to analyze the particular audience to whom he would be speaking, namely, his classmates. As he began his speech with the following question, "How many of you drive to campus to get to your classes?", he anticipated a large number of students to nod in agreement or perhaps even raise their hands. Unfortunately, he was met with puzzled looks instead because this particular class was made up mostly of freshmen who aren't allowed to have cars on campus and who all used the bus system already! It was a painful eight minutes listening to him try and convince the audience to do what they were already doing – ride the bus around campus.

Using a question to attain the attention of your listeners need not involve their standing, raising hands, or answering out loud. **Rhetorical** questions are asked without expectation of a response, usually to create a certain effect within the audience. Rhetorical questions can be effective in attaining an audience's attention IF you have confidence your listeners will answer (silently or otherwise) in the way that you expect.

Share a startling fact or statistic. Providing a startling fact or statistic can draw the audience's attention by jolting them out of complacency. For example, one student began her speech on clean drinking water this way:

I see several of you brought water or something else to drink to class today. How long did it take you to get that drink? Probably not very long. We basically can get clean water whenever we want it, but in many areas of the world this is not the case. In countries that lack access to clean water, women and girls spend up to six hours daily collecting water. That's more time than a student taking a normal load spends in class on a daily basis!

This method of capturing an audience's attention is most effective when not overplayed. Don't present your example or comparison in an overly dramatic way. Present the facts in a straightforward, clear, and compelling manner. Often when we start with a startling fact or statistic, we need to pause and let what we have said "sink in" for our audience members. The idea is to cause your audience to reflect.

Use a relevant quotation. Starting a speech with a relevant quotation can provide a theme or frame to the rest of your speech. Often speakers will use a quotation from someone famous, but the most important point is that the quotation be relevant to your speech. Starting with John F. Kennedy's famous "Ask not what your country can do for you; ask what you can do for your country." might make sense in a speech about volunteering, but be less relevant to a speech on spring break vacations. Where can we find useful quotations? Of course we can search the Internet for "famous quotations," but did you know there are actually books that compile this information for you? Check out Barlett's Famous Quotations or The Oxford Dictionary of Quotations in the reference section of your library. These books do the hard work for you and organize quotations by author, including ancient, modern, and pop culture sources.

Tell a humorous story or joke. The first rule of joke and humorous story telling is what I like to call "the grandma rule." If you wouldn't tell the story or joke to your grandmother, you probably shouldn't tell it to the class! Just as you would do with quotations, keep the story short, simple, and relevant. Also keep in mind that an attention-getter should utilize your strengths as a speaker. If you routinely forget the punch line when telling jokes to your friends, this may not be the opener for you! Just as you can with quotations, jokes can be found in books, magazines, and online, but should be relevant to the speech. For example, when my daughter ran for a position in student government at her school, her speech emphasized her skills as a problem-solver. She decided to open her speech with a relevant joke: "What did one math book say to the other? We've got problems!" Be sure your joke is clean, easy to deliver, and relevant to the topic.

Use a real or hypothetical illustration. An illustration could be a real story, or a story from literature, or even just a plausible tale. Like our other options for drawing the attention of an audience, the story must be relevant to the main point of your speech. Such stories can come from newspapers, magazines, sermons, and your own life experiences. For example, one student used just such a story when giving her informative speech:

I'm leaving a late night movie with my father when suddenly, as he's driving, we hear it and see it. Those dreaded lights and sirens! My father pulls over and the police officer politely asks him if he's been drinking. With slurred speech, and the smell of alcohol on his breath, my father responds, "No, officer." In that moment, if my father had been arrested for drunk driving, he could have died. You see, my father wasn't drunk, but slipping into diabetic shock. Nearly 29 million people in America are diabetics. Today I'm going to share with you some information about diabetes: its causes, symptoms, and treatments.

This student used a personal illustration to great effect. She attained the attention of the audience by drawing them in with a story that was true, personal, and cleverly told.

Step Two: Reveal the topic

Once you have attained audience's attention, you can move on to framing the content of your speech. A Specific Purpose Statement is a clear, short, declarative statement that presents the main idea of your speech. Too often speakers will "bury the lead" by having a long, detailed sentence for their main idea, and before they can get to the end, they've lost the attention of the audience. Your Specific Purpose should be clear and concise. To generate this statement, think about what you want your audience to know or understand after you have spoken. That's your specific purpose. Leave no doubt in listeners' minds exactly what you will be speaking about: "Today I will share with you the benefits of learning a foreign language in college."

Step Three: Relate to the audience (WIIFM)

In many speaking situations, making sure your audience knows why they are listening to the speech is an essential step to getting them to listen. A statement of relevance explains why the knowledge to be gained through the speech is important to the speaker and should be important to the audience. Think about the illustration about the diabetic man above. Although the story is dramatic, it may not seem important to you. Adding in the evidence that 29 million people in the US are diabetic helps to raise the significance of the topic. Making one more statement — that with current levels of diabetes in the U.S., odds are very likely you already know someone with diabetes, or may even be at risk for developing diabetes- would relate the topic to you more closely. That connection between the topic and the audience is an essential part of an effective speech. Letting your audience know what they will get out of your speech increases your chances of holding their attention.

"WIIFM" stands for "What's In It For Me?" This is a crucial question that effective speakers must clearly answer for their audience. After revealing yoiur topic clearly, you can further enhance your credibility by explaining to the audience how listening to your speech will benefit them; how the information you share will be relevant to their lives.

Step Four: Establish credibility

It's important to establish for your audience why you are a credible speaker. Explaining to your audience how you gained expertise in your topic may seem a bit uncomfortable at first. Often in the "real world" speakers are introduced by others who share and explain the speaker's credibility with the audience. However, we must become comfortable providing our credentials on our own behalf. This sets the audience expectation that you have solid, important information to share, and that you are well-versed in your speech topic. However, we must remember that credibility is perceived by the listeners. Even being a Ph.D. (presumably an expert) on a topic does not guarantee that audience members will find a speaker credible. What exactly, then, does it take for an audience to grant a speaker credibility? To answer this question, let's return to the roots of the communication discipline: Aristotle. Aristotle divided the art of persuasion into three main components — pathos (emotion), logos (logic), and ethos (character/credibility). Establishing one's ethos is multi-faceted. Audiences need to know

if they can respect you, if you are generally trustworthy, and if you can speak on your subject with authority. To help establish your credibility, inform the audience of your preparation and readiness to speak on the subject. (See also Chapter 5, especially the sections on verbal and non-verbal cues.)

Step Five: Preview the body of the speech

The final step is to preview the main points to be covered in the body of the speech. To remain with the topic statement just introduced above, once you know the speech is about benefits of learning a foreign language, it is important to briefly lay out how you plan to discuss those benefits, and how many benefits will be discussed. The preview statement helps listeners stay on track and follow the speaker: "I want to share with you three benefits of learning a foreign language while in college: enhanced cognitive function, improved multitasking, and increased employability upon graduation." Be careful not to give too much detail in your preview – you want to keep it brief. Your audience should know where you're headed but the details get delivered in the body of your speech.

Thoughtfully developing and including all five steps in your introduction sets up the optimal situation for your speech to be most effective. Each step connects to the next so you have a strong, smooth beginning to your presentation. By gaining the attention of your audience, clearly stating your topic, relating your topic to the audience, establishing your credibility, and previewing the body of the speech, you have created a situation where your audience is attentive, engaged, and ready to hear more. As a bonus for most speakers, their speech anxiety peaks and then falls dramatically after about 30 seconds of speaking. A five step introduction takes just about 30-60 seconds to deliver. By the time you're ready for the body of your speech, you'll be feeling much less anxious and more able to focus on your message.

Be sure to include all five steps for an effective introduction: gaining the attention of your audience, clearly stating your topic, relating your topic to the audience, establishing your credibility, and previewing the body of the speech.

Conclusions – The End

Like introductions, conclusions are often neglected by the speaker. Students sometimes end speeches by thanking the audience for their time, or asking for questions, but these are not truly effective endings. A solid conclusion reviews the main points of the speech and leaves the audience with a sense of closure. In order to prepare an effective conclusion, a speaker should do the following when preparing a conclusion:

Step One: Signal that the speech is ending.

A transitional word or phrase, such as "finally," or "to conclude my speech," usually precedes the ending of a speech. The section on transitions, in Chapter 9, will address this question in greater detail. You can also repeat the specific purpose statement to remind the audience about the main purpose of your speech.

Step Two: Reinforce the central idea of the speech/Summarize the the main points.

Remember this is akin to a thesis statement in the paper. Repeating the basics of your main points helps cement them in the minds of your audience.

Your conclusion creates the final impression in the minds of your audience. Don't leave it to chance. Carefully plan out your conclusion and practice it so you are ready to leave a forceful and lasting impression on your audience. Once you signal to your audience that your speech will soon be ending, it's important to summarize your main points.

Additional Ideas for a Good Conclusion

Figure 7.2

- Provide an appropriate quotation
- Challenge your audience to do something
- Return to a story or joke from your introduction

Provide an appropriate quotation. Similar to gaining the attention of the audience in your introduction, you can use a quotation to bring a note of finality to your speech. For example, a speech about the benefits of active listening might end with the proverb: "We have two ears and one mouth, because listening is twice as important as talking." A brief and relevant quotation at the end of a speech can stir an audience and help them reflect on the information you have just shared.

Challenge your audience. Particularly when doing a persuasive speech, a challenge to the audience to do something can make for an effective and emotional conclusion. For example, if a speaker is trying to persuade the audience to get involved in the worldwide lack of clean drinking water, a challenge to the audience to donate the money they typically spend on bottled water in a week could be an effective call to action.

Return to a story or joke from the introduction. Returning to a story or joke you mentioned in your introduction provides coherence to your speech. One student gave a speech on the problem of human trafficking and started her speech this way:

> 43,200. That's the number Karla Jacinto told the CNN reporter to remember. It's the number of times Karla was raped during her time in captivity due to human trafficking. That's 30 men per day, seven days a week, for almost four years.

After giving a stirring and disturbing informative speech on the current state of human trafficking, the student returned to Karla's story for the conclusion:

> Karla is now 23 years old. She's told her story to the United States Congress, the Pope at the Vatican, and speaks out at conferences and events aimed at stopping human trafficking. Karla is one of the lucky ones. She escaped. Won't you get involved to help others like Karla?

These three strategies for ending the speech with the appropriate mood can be used separately or together. Your conclusion creates the final impression in the minds of your audience. Don't leave it to chance. Carefully plan out your conclusion and practice it so you are ready to leave a forceful and lasting impression.

8
The Preparation Outline

Dr. Sandra French
Radford University

When crafting your speech, you will likely use two types of outlines – the preparation outline and the speaking outline. The speaking outline you will learn about in Chapter 13.

In this chapter you will learn how to create a thorough preparation outline for your speech. An effective outline will help you gather and organize your thoughts so that you can clearly present your topic to the audience.

Think of your outline as a structure that will support your speech. We are living in an era with access to more information than at any other time in history, and unless we properly understand and implement outlining, our message risks being lost in a deluge of that information. Information found on the Internet can be read over and over to increase comprehension, but a speech unfolds moment-by-moment for an audience. A well-placed car horn, a missed lunch, a conflict with a co-worker, or a momentary daydream, any of these might prevent an audience member from following the message a speaker is trying to convey. Because we are so prone to distraction, both from within and without, effective outlining is crucial to effective public communication. An effective speech is organized in such a way as to repeatedly emphasize the main points for listeners; even if attention wavers, they can easily rejoin the speaker's message and fill in the gaps. Think of outlining as a gift you give to your audience to give them the best possible chance of really hearing what you have to say.

After thoroughly researching a topic, a speaker must have a clear understanding of what they want to share with the audience. Outlining helps a speaker to see connections between their research materials and to pick out quotations or examples that are likely to have the biggest impact on the audience. Most importantly, outlining provides clarity and helps a speaker stay on topic and make the information more understandable. The preparation outline is written in complete sentences and fully encapsulates the topic you plan to present. The crafting of a preparation outline is like the piecing together of a puzzle; the key is figuring out where all the pieces of information fit and how they fit together in the bigger scheme of things.

The Preparation Outline

The preparation outline, true to its name, helps you to prepare your presentation. This is the stage at which you will try out several different organizational patterns to find the best approach to sharing your information. At this stage, you will also finalize your thesis statement and experiment with different main points based on your research and the speaking situation. You should be prepared to do a lot of reorganizing and rearranging of information. Remember, the preparation outline is like a puzzle, where the presenter tries out different pieces of information in different places to find the perfect fit for a given purpose and audience.

Visual Framework: Labels, Symbols and Indentations

A good preparation outline begins with a clear and well-organized visual framework consisting of labels, symbols, and indentations. Variations to this framework exist but the most common is detailed below.

Labels

The outline should consist of three main sections labeled **Introduction, Body and Conclusion.** These labels themselves don't get assigned Roman numerals. They are typically positioned closest to the left margin.

Symbols

A numeric-alpha system is employed to mark the main points, sub-points, and sub sub-points of the outline. Main points are denoted by Roman numerals. Capital letters are used to identify sub-points. Sub sub-points are identified by Arabic numbers.

Indentations

Through indenting the smaller ideas you create a hierarchy of importance and precedence within the visual framework of the outline. In addition, consistent and correct use of indentations will provide a logical continuity to the flow of information and how that information is expressed.

For an example of this visual framework see Figure 8.2 later in this chapter.

Criteria for Content of an Effective Preparation Outline

Full Sentences

The preparation outline is written in full sentences. There should be one sentence per symbol except in the case of multi-sentence quotes and grouped statistics. Your preparation outline should also include transitions; well-thought out sentences that move an audience from one main point to the next, or one part of the speech to the next.

Symmetry in Rhetoric

Symmetry in rhetoric is not about language. It is about creating balance within the visual framework of your outline. There must be at least two of each symbol to maintain this balance. For example, in the sample preparation outline found later in this chapter, you will note that each main point consists of two sub-points and each sub-point consists of two sub sub-points. This helps to establish a proper and logical balance between all the points conveyed.

Balancing Main Points

An important corresponding principle is to keep your main points in balance. In other words, for a speech with three main points you should try and provide a similar amount of information in each main point; it shouldn't take three minutes to cover main point one, seven minutes to cover main point two, and four minutes to cover main point three.

To begin your preparation outline, start with your general purpose – is this a speech to inform, persuade, or entertain? Next, craft the main idea (sometimes called the specific purpose statement) of the speech.

Figure 8.1 **Keys to Creating an Effective**

1. **Start with your General and Specific Purpose**

2. **Identify and Label the Introduction, Speech Body, and Conclusion**

3. **Use Labels and Symbols to create a Visual Framework that will help you to structure your speech**

4. **Create a Main Point/Subpoint, Sub-subpoint Structure (see Figure 8.2 'Sample Outline')**

5. **Use full sentences to fully encapsulate the ideas that you are planning to present.**

6. **Include formal citations in your outline. By using signal phrases, also known as introductory phrases, within the text of the outline as opposed to citing all of your source information parenthetically, your oral citations will be easier to include on the speaking outline.**

General Purpose-To Inform.

Specific Purpose Statement: To inform my audience about strokes.

Now that you have articulated your general and specific purpose, it is time to begin writing the preparation outline. Remember to follow outline form and to write in full sentences. If any individual component takes more than one sentence, subpoints should be used. Your preparation outline is a visual framework of your talking points and their relationship to one another, so be sure and use not only the symbols associated with outlining format. When outlining, be sure to follow proper indentation. Indenting provides consistency and helps clarify the relationship between your points. Be sure that text is under text (not under an outlining symbol) and that you follow the subject of your previous sentence. See the Sample Preparation Outline with labels later on in this chapter for further assistance.

Once the preparation outline is written, use it to gauge whether your speech successfully meets the criteria of the assignment. Read through your preparation outline as if you were delivering your speech. Is it too long? Too short? Take note of how long it takes you to read through each main point. Are the main points out of balance, either in terms of content, complexity, or time needed for delivery? Remember that you want to keep each main point within a similar time frame so that your points are not out of balance.

Read through your preparation outline several times, using the following questions to guide you as you assess its effectiveness:

- Are my main points clear?

  - If you read through your preparation outline for a friend and they cannot easily pick out your main points and repeat them back to you, see how you can better emphasize them. Repetition of main ideas is key to helping them stand out to an audience.

  - Do I use complete sentences?

– Do I restrict myself to one sentence per symbol (exception: multi-sentence quotes and grouped statistics)

• Are my supporting materials clear and supported?

– Am I orally citing my sources?

– Do I have at least one source to support each main point?

While your individual speaking assignments will vary, most preparation outlines should include these components. In Chapter 13, you can find a full length example of a Preparation Outline, complete with full sentences.

Figure 8.2 **Sample Outline: Sample Outline Structure**

General Purpose:

Specific Purpose Statement:

Introduction

      I. Attain the attention of the audience (one sentence)

      II. Reveal topic, stating the one main idea of the speech (one sentence)

      III. Relate to the audience (one sentence)

      IV. Establish credibility

      V. Preview of Main Points (one sentence)

Transition to Speech Body (one sentence)

Speech Body

I. Main Point One

    A. Subpoint

        1. Sub-subpoint

        2. Sub-subpoint

    B. Subpoint

        1. Sub-subpoint

        2. Sub-subpoint

II. Main Point Two

    A. Subpoint

        1. Sub-subpoint

        2. Sub-subpoint

    B. Subpoint

        1. Sub-subpoint

        2. Sub-subpoint

Conclusion

I. Signal that the Speech is Coming to a Close.

II. Restatement of the Central Idea

Critical Thinking Questions

A public speaker should use a series of critical thinking questions to help him or her to create the preparation outline. You must make sure that the audience understands your main points. If an event happens it's not enough to just state that it happened. You have to ask yourself, where it happened, who it happened to, why it happened, how it happened, who said it happened, and lastly, how do you know who said it. This line of questioning will help you to find your sub-points and sub sub-points and let you know when and where you must indent.

Bibliography

The last component of a preparation outline is a complete reference list, created according to the assignment specifics and including all relevant information so that your sources can easily be found by others. Most instructors will suggest a standard style for citations, such as APA, MLA, or Chicago. Be sure to check the assignment specifics and provide the reference list in the appropriate format. Your library or writing center is a good place to obtain assistance for compiling adequate citations.

The function and purpose of the bibliography is an act of generosity from the scholar. As always, it is important to cite works that you used to help create your speech. Your sources should also be cited in a page that follows your outline. Internet articles, books, interviews, and newspaper articles must all be properly cited if they helped you to formulate your ideas. The most common formats for citing sources are APA (American Psychological Association) and MLA (Modern Language Association).

Oral Citation: Sources should be cited within the outline, just as you plan to say them during your speech. Your sources should also be cited in a page that follows your outline.

9

Constructing the Body of the Speech

Dr. Sandra French
Radford University

As you continue to work on structuring your speech in a manner that clearly relates your central idea to your audience you will want to present your main points in the body of your speech. The number of main point sentences depends on the manner in which your speech is organized. Many speeches have between two and five main points. Main points are then supported by sub-points and sub sub-points supported by sub-points and sub sub-points just as they are in your preparation outline. The body of the speech is where you apply organizational models to help you arrange your speech.

Speech Body: A Review of Organizational Models with Examples

When crafting his or her main points, a speaker must decide how to arrange them. Effective organization of supporting materials provides a logical and smooth flow to a speech. Speeches that are well-organized are easier for the speaker to deliver and for the audience to understand. Again, a speaker needs to ask one main question, *"What's the best way for me to show the relationships between my materials?"* In answering this question, a speaker will often clearly decide on one of five organizational patterns.

Figure 9.1 **Organizational Patterns**

It is important to note that the same topic, organized differently, will produce a drastically different speech. Later in this chapter, we will see how speeches about the same topic can look quite different and provide much different information, depending on which organizational pattern we choose.

Pay particular attention to which organizational patterns are most appropriate for informative and persuasive speeches.

Chronological. A chronologically organized speech is one arranged according to time. This organizational pattern works well for **informative speeches** that take an audience through the history of a person, place, or idea. For example, a speech about the life of a historical figure like Harry Truman lends itself to a chronological organizational pattern, with main points easily divided into periods of time.

SPECIFIC PURPOSE STATEMENT: To inform my audience about Harry S. Truman's path to the presidency.

BODY:

I.   After serving as a captain in the Field Artillery during World War I Truman became active in the Democratic party.

II.   In 1922, Truman was elected to the administrative position as judge of the Jackson County Court.

III.   In 1934, he was elected as a Democratic Senator representing Missouri.

IV.   In 1944, President Roosevelt chose Truman as his running mate.

V.   In 1945, when Franklin Roosevelt died, Truman took over the presidency.

This chronological organizational pattern arranges Truman's life in an order based on time. This takes the listener through his unlikely rise to the presidency. Other organizational patterns might include some of the same research, but may have a different focus as needed.

Spatial. A spatial organizational pattern follows a direction. A spatially organized speech, in effect, makes you the tour guide for your audience. An informative speech about the Pyramids at Giza, for example, could be arranged spatially as you take your audience through each separate archaeological site, or on a tour of one particular pyramid like the Great Pyramid.

SPECIFIC PURPOSE STATEMENT: To inform my audience of the Pyramids at Giza

BODY:

I.   The largest of the three pyramids at Giza, known as the Great Pyramid, is the funery complex of Khufu, the son of King Sneferu.

II.   The middle sized pyramid at Giza was built by Khufu's son, Khafre.

III.   The smallest pyramid at Giza was built by Khafre's son, Menkaura.

The spatial organizational structure works well for describing some kind of landscape, such as a theme park, the D-day beaches of the Normandy Invasion, or an archaeological site.

Topical. Topical organizational structure, where you divide a larger subject into logical sub-topics, is the most commonly used organizational method and works for any type of speech. There is no right or wrong way to divide a topic; just use ways that makes sense given your main purpose for the speech. The more logically you organize your ideas the easier it will be for the audience to follow along and understand your message.

SPECIFIC PURPOSE STATEMENT: To inform my audience of wedding rituals in China.

BODY:

I. There are pre-wedding rituals that are done by both the bride and groom's families.

II. The day of the wedding includes many rituals for the bride and groom.

III. There are many post-wedding rituals of a Chinese wedding.

Notice the logical structure to the speech body and that each main point is an independent idea. The topical organizational structure can be used for almost any subject and is the most frequently used of all five organizational patterns.

Cause-Effect. This pattern of organization is particularly useful when giving **persuasive speeches,** as it shows the relationship between various conditions and their impacts. While it is possible to use this organizational structure for *informative speeches,* one must take care when discussing effects not to transition into telling the audience what to do. For example, if the purpose of one's speech is to inform the audience about skin cancer, the cause-effect structure could work well:

SPECIFIC PURPOSE STATEMENT: To inform my audience about skin cancer.

BODY

I. There are three major causes of skin cancer.

II. Skin cancer affects the body in different ways.

When using the Cause-Effect structure, a speaker might choose to first discuss various causes (reasons) then explain their effects (consequences). However, a speaker can also discuss the effects first and explain the causes second. Suppose you were giving a speech about the lack of worldwide access to childhood vaccines. Your speech might start with the effects of non-vaccination and then discuss the reasons why vaccinations are not readily available worldwide.

Problem-Solution. The problem-solution structure divides a speech into two main sections: a discussion of the problem (or problems) and a discussion of the solution. This organizational structure is used primarily in *persuasive speaking,* as the speaker's purpose is usually to convince the audience to support or engage in some type of action to alleviate a problem. The speaker attempts to convince an audience that a problem exists, and then to convince that audience to change either a pattern of thought, an attitude, or a behavior as part of the solution. In the first section, a speaker uses their research to demonstrate to the audience that a problem exists, and show its different facets, its impact, and seriousness. In the second section, the speaker identifies a potential solution to the problem and shows how the audience can participate in making the solution a reality. For example, in crafting a speech about the problem of obesity in America, the outline for the speech body might look like this:

SPECIFIC PURPOSE STATEMENT: To persuade my audience that eating healthier should be made easier.

BODY

    I.   The rising levels of obesity are creating problems.

        A. One problem is that medical issues are increasing in children.

        B. A second problem is that obese adults are dying at an earlier age.

    II.   The plan I propose is to make eating healthier a way of life.

        A. The first part of the plan is to have more nutritional food served in schools.

        B. The second part of the plan is to teach better eating habits to school children.

It is not mandatory to have the same number of sub-points in the problem and solution; just be sure to adequately address each of them. However, exceeding three sub-points may give the audience more supporting material than they can remember.

Connectives

Even the most logically organized speech needs connections to help the speech flow from one point to the next. These connections are known as **connectives,** or words and phrases that signal to the audience when a speaker is changing between main points or between main sections of a speech (from introduction to speech body to conclusion). Proper use of connectives helps a speech flow smoothly and assists the audience in following a speaker's logical progression of ideas.

Transitions are complete sentences that appear before and between main points and help the audience to follow the organizational pattern of the speech. These verbal cues alert the audience about a move from one completed thought or idea to a new one. One example of this sort of transition is a properly placed question. Questions invite answers and invite the audience to silently or subliminally follow along to receive those answers. For example, in a speech on identity theft a speaker could introduce a main point with the following question: "So just how prevalent are skimming devices?" This lets the audience know what will be covered in the next main point and prepares the audience to receive the answer to the question.

Like Transitions, **Signposting** signals that a transition is taking place. While transitions are complete sentences, Signposts are typically little words or groups of words. "The <u>first</u> symptom of skin cancer is...; The <u>second</u> symptom is...." Other examples of Signpost words are: next, finally, to the north, etc. Speakers often use a combination of Transitions and Signposting to make sure that the audience stays engaged and follows along with the speaker into each new part of the expression of his or her message.

Here are some useful signpost words and phrases:

Figure 9.2

- **Time-related: soon, meanwhile, then, after**

- **Contrasting: nevertheless, but, so, although**

- **Additive: also, furthermore, in addition**

- **Concluding: finally, to summarize, in conclusion, to review**

A second type of connective is **internal previews** and **summaries**. An internal preview or summary introduces or reviews multiple points and provides a link to the next point. "Now that I have told you about the prevalence of skin cancer and the importance of sunscreen, let's talk about what ingredients to look for in sunscreen products." Such a sentence assists the audience in remembering the points you have already covered and how they connect to the material left to be shared.

Try not to get bogged down in what type of connective you are using. Just remember that it is important to include connectives and that they help make a speech more understandable to your audience.

References

Crano, William A. (1977). "Primacy versus Recency in Retention of Information and Opinion Change." *The Journal of Social Psychology.* 101(1) pp.87-96. DOI: 10.1080/00224545.1977.9923987

Goman, Carol. (2011). "7 Seconds to Make A First Impression." *Forbes.* http://www.forbes.com/sites/carolkinseygoman/2011/02/13/seven-seconds-to-make-a-firstimpression/#3c9a8724645a

Jobs, Steve. (2005). Stanford Commencement Address. http://news.stanford.edu/2005/06/14/jobs-061505/

Nieuwhof, Carey. (2015). "7 Easy Ways to Ruin an Otherwise Great Sermon, Message or Talk (And How to Fix It)." http://careynieuwhof. com/2015/01/7-ways-ruinotherwise-great-sermon-message-talk-fix/

Zug, George. *Encyclopedia Britannica.* "Asp." https://www.britannica.com/animal/aspas

10

Research for Effective Communication

Dr. Tracey Quigley Holden
University of Delaware

Introduction

Research can be defined as "the strategic acquisition of information." Being a good researcher means being aware of what you want your audience to know by the end of your speech. It means understanding the information gap between your knowledge of a given topic and what you need to know in order to communicate your message to your audience. Knowing the proper techniques of research will help to fill that gap in both informative and persuasive speeches.

There are three main aspects of the research process: **gathering** information, **assessing** information, and **placing** information.

In gathering information it is important to be aware of proper search terms relating to your topic. It is also important not to use the usual mainstream databases like Google and Wikipedia. Instead, it is recommended that you use reputable scholarly databases.

Assessing the information you gather means evaluating your evidence using multiple criteria, choosing a variety of types of evidence, and being able to know and to cite your sources. **Statistics, examples,** and **testimony** are the main types of evidence you can choose when assessing information. Given the speed of change in our digital age it is often the case that what was considered accurate information a year ago has become obsolete. Therefore, it is usually preferable to assess the most recent information and data when conducting your research. Another crucial aspect of this process is the consideration of whether or not the information you gather is relevant to your topic.

Finally, the researcher places the information into the format of a speech or presentation that starts with an introduction, is followed by main points, and ends with a conclusion. It is good to remember when placing data that seven is the ideal number of pieces of information that an audience can recall.

Continue reading to find out more about research techniques and the importance of using research to help you inform and persuade an audience.

Public speakers, especially politicians, are often accused of offering their audiences nothing but hot air—lots of words and energy, but little content. In order to be an effective speaker, you must have more than enough information about your chosen topic to share with your audience. The way to find that information is to do research. Research might sound difficult or intimidating, but it is something you do every day—you gather information about topics you're interested in so you can make better choices. If you were considering taking a job, buying a car, or getting a roommate, you would spend time gathering and assessing information about your options. That is research! Research for a presentation should be more thorough and more selective than deciding on a restaurant to eat in this weekend, but both tasks involve the strategic acquisition of information.

In many train stations, metro stations, and even airports around the world, you will see signs and hear announcements telling you to "Mind the Gap." The gap in a train station is the space between the train and the platform, something you need to be aware of so you can cross it safely to get where you're going. One way to think about the information you need for your speech is to recognize existing "information gaps" you need to cross in order to effectively reach your audience. As you begin researching your topic, there is an information gap between what you know at the start and what you need to know for your speech. There is also an information gap between you and your audience when you begin to present your speech. The gap between what you know, think, and believe about your topic and what your audience knows, thinks, and believes is the gap that you want to bridge with the information you choose to include in your presentation. Recognizing these information gaps helps you to think through the process of research and begin to identify the information you need. You need to "Mind the Gap!"

If you want to bridge an information gap, you will need to:

Gather the information you need about your topic;

Assess the information you find to determine its accuracy, quality, and appropriateness for your presentation;

Place the information in your presentation strategically, so your audience has the best opportunity to understand your ideas.

Gathering Information

If you have ever felt like there was just too much information to take in, let alone to sort through, you are not alone. As far back as the 1660s, people began to notice and complain about how much information was available. The term "information society" has become a common way of describing our current culture, and the burden of "information overload" is one we all carry. The concept of the information society emerged early in the 20th century, as the rate of expansion of human knowledge approached an exponential pace. In the 1970s, the term "information society" first appeared as the economic impact of human knowledge and its distribution began to overtake production of goods (Crawford, 1983). In the years since the term was coined, the rate of information production and dissemination has only increased. A 2015 IBM research article cites industry analysts projecting a data growth rate of 800% over the next five years, or nearly doubling every 12 months (Kelly, 2015).

Research is done using **primary** and **secondary** sources. Primary sources are the original documents from history, or accounts or materials produced by people with firsthand experience. Secondary sources are interpretations or analyses produced by people who did not have the experience themselves. Most of your research will be with primary sources. Of course, you can do your own **original** research as well. Speakers are sometimes able to **survey** their audiences to gain relevant information prior to a speech, such as audience knowledge about and attitudes toward a given subject. **Interviews** could be conducted by the speaker to obtain firsthand accounts and comments from the people with relevant experience or expertise with a topic area.

Interviews

Interviewing an expert can be one of the best ways to do research. There are two important considerations when conducting interviews — finding an expert, and asking good questions. The key to finding an expert is considering their qualifications as you do for any source. Does the person have specific, relevant, expert knowledge about your topic? Can you translate that knowledge into material that is understandable for your audience? Is the expert willing to meet with you? Before you ask for an interview, you need to research the expert and develop a set of questions. Questions should not ask the expert to recount basic information about themselves or their area of expertise; that is material you should already know from your research. A good question is specific, relevant to your topic, and gives the expert room to provide details or a story about their work. For example, if you have the chance to meet with a U.S. government official, it's not useful to ask them about the U.S. withdrawal from the Paris Agreement, you will get a stock answer. Instead, ask something like, "Have scientists at the EPA changed their approach to climate change research?" or "What do you see as the most effective path forward to deal with climate change?" The last two questions give the expert some room to answer and ask for something beyond a yes or no.

Digital/Internet Research

No matter how you look at it, there is a colossal amount of information available. This makes an effective strategy for gathering information one of the most important aspects of research. Thinking ahead and doing a little advance planning will significantly reduce the time you spend gathering information, as well as improve the quality of the information you get. The saying, "Five minutes of planning is worth fifteen minutes of just looking" applies even more today than when E.L. Konigsburg wrote it in 1967. There are three steps to effective, strategic information gathering, and each one is described below.

1. Choose your search terms carefully.

2. Use the best available search tools.

3. Use your results to refine your search further.

Choose Your Search Terms Carefully

For a search to be effective, it should be focused and tailored to produce high quality results. Starting with good search terms – the words and parameters you search for – is a critical step to finding good information. Knowing the topic you want to search for is a good starting point, but knowing a couple of related terms or possible sub-topics is even better. Too broad a topic or search term will return too many results. Take five minutes to write down the key word or central phrase of your topic, and then add another three to five terms that are either directly related to your topic or indicate another area you are considering. For example, if your topic is "student activities," you might add "sports," "recreation," and "Greek life." Or you could start with "student activities" and add "funding," "diversity," and "campus culture". Using a combination of keywords and phrases will help you focus on your topic, and will generate a stronger set of results from any search.

Usually a search will produce more results than you can use. But if you don't get enough results, or if the initial results don't seem clearly related to your topic, you need another approach. This is when the concept of related terms can help you. For this purpose Boolean operators are your friends. If your initial key word doesn't produce results, look for a synonym or a related term. In the example above, "student activities" was the prime key word. Another closely related term would be "student organizations" or "college clubs." Changing your terms can produce very different results. It is important to keep in mind that the same topic can have several different names, and a simple change of terms could connect you to better resources. Boolean operators are the short words that connect your search terms into a searchable string; AND, OR, and NOT are used in most cases, with AND NOT is used occasionally. Here is how they work when you have two related terms:

AND — tells the search engine to look for BOTH terms: (Dogs AND Cats).

OR — tells the search engine to look for EITHER term: (Dogs OR Cats).

NOT — tells the search engine to look for the first term, but exclude items containing both the first and second term: (Dogs NOT Cats).

A search done using "prison reading programs" and one done using "prison AND reading programs" could produce very different results within the same search engine. Substituting "correctional institution" for "prison" produces another set of results. Trying "literacy" OR "reading" produces still another. As you work through your terms and combinations, you are likely to see the same articles show up in multiple searches. Those are the articles you look at first, to see if you are getting the kind of results you need.

Use The Best Available Search Tools

Search mechanisms such as Google and Wikipedia can provide you with a lot of information and sources to check, but they will also turn up a lot of junk and information from unknown, unverifiable, or poor quality sources.

A better option is to use a search engine which curates and reviews the indexed information. Google offers "Google Scholar" as a public access, but limited-content search engine which focuses on scholarly articles in recognized journals across a wide range of topic areas and scholarly disciplines. Elsevier, Oxford University Press, Science Direct, and Wiley are all publishers of open access journals. Depending on your topic, searching in a scholarly and open access database could be very helpful to you. The articles and journals in these databases are usually peer-reviewed which means experts in the field have read and approved the content. This can offer you a much higher caliber of information, especially for technical topics. Along the same lines, most industries have professional associations and publications within their field that offer well-edited, relevant information. These organizations and publications are geared toward people already working in that area who need to stay aware of important trends and innovations. If you are working on a related topic, or have a strong interest in a particular industry, you should find out which sources professionals in the field use to stay up to date.

If you have access to a good library, especially a college or university library, you may be able to use a database to do your search. This is almost always your best option for high quality information. Some databases, such as Lexis-Nexus or General OneFile, are wide-ranging, covering a huge range of topics across thousands of sources in popular media or publicly accessible records. Other databases, such as ProQuest and Academic OneFile, cover a wide range of topics and areas of knowledge but prioritize scholarly journals in their search.

There are many databases that are more specialized, covering a limited number of scholarly sources in a particular discipline. JSTOR indexes the contents of scholarly journals in the social sciences, including history, sociology, and political science. There are databases that only index newspapers, databases that index business and company information, and databases for science and medical information. The New York Times has digitized access to almost all of its issues going back to 1851, including the advertisements.

Databases such as these offer access to high quality information, often within a particular area of knowledge, and can include the most cutting edge and recent research. Working in these databases can require patience and persistence. Unlike Google, where you can type in anything you want and start searching, scholarly databases often require you to set careful search parameters before you can start looking. There can be layers of menu options to select from and multiple search terms to enter. Often you can set a specific date range, request only full text and/or peer reviewed articles be included, even search for court cases or government proceedings. The process takes some getting used to, and what works in one database will not always work in another, but the overall quality of information is well worth the time. Remember also that the Camden County College website has a link to the library and to your professor's library guide, both having a number of recommended scholarly databases and resources.

Use Your Results to Refine Your Search Further

Once you have begun searching, there are several things you can do to help narrow and focus your results and sift out the best quality information. As you are looking at a results list, keep in mind that most people never get beyond page 2. Take a look at how your results are reported. Many search engines and databases default to a ranking by "relevance" but how that affects your results can vary. It could merely mean that the items at the top of the results had the most occurrences of your search terms. Viewing your results with different sorting criteria, perhaps in chronological order from newest to oldest, can help you identify the most current information.

Keeping track of items you have found that you want to review in more depth is a must. If you are searching using a public search engine, it helps to open a file for notes and a folder for saving documents on your computer as you are searching. If you are able to open a file, keep a running list of the titles, authors, and if possible, links to the most promising items. If you identify a document or an article that you want to review more carefully, download it and save it where you can find it later. Most databases have a way to tag or mark items for later review – take advantage of that option if it is available. In some cases, you can have items emailed directly to you. Make sure the notes about your items are complete enough such that you can locate them again. As search parameters change and as the search engines 'learn' what you're looking for, you can lose earlier items. Losing track of a good article is frustrating, and too often it is impossible to recreate the search.

As you identify and review items, you can dig into them for additional nuggets of information. In scholarly articles, and some Wikipedia entries, there are links and lists of references to earlier research or related articles. Especially in scholarly articles, those reference lists can lead you to the most important, earliest, or most reputable research in the area. They can also lead to controversial issues and differences within a field. Either way, you have gained information and insight into your topic.

Each of these strategies can and should be repeated until you have a reasonably large number of possible items to review. It is up to you to decide what is enough material to work with before you search again or move on to the next step. Putting time and effort into the information gathering part of preparation is essential. As the saying goes, Garbage In, Garbage Out! Without good information to choose from, your presentation will not reflect positively on you as a speaker, nor will it help you bridge the gap to your audience. It's also helpful to review a few articles at a time, rather than trying to plow through a giant stack. Knowing what you have and what you still need can help you search more effectively.

Assessing Information

When you have gathered several articles or sources you are ready to review, take a minute to consider what your goals are for your presentation. What do you want your audience to know, believe, or do after you speak? Having a clear sense of your goals as a speaker will help you look for the specific information you will use in your presentation.

The articles and other items you have gathered are basically raw information. What you want to pull out of that material is evidence. Evidence is the information you use to support the major claims and ideas in your presentation. There are multiple types of evidence you can use, and each type adds something a little different to your presentation. However, all good evidence can stand up to close inspection, and all evidence should meet basic evaluative criteria before any of it is included in your presentation. Evidence also requires attribution – you have to let your audience know where you got it and who wrote or created it. Failing to provide correct and appropriate citations for your evidence is plagiarism – a form of theft which can have serious consequences. These three practices will help you identify the best information to include in your presentation.

Figure 10.1 **Three Practices...**

1. **Evaluate the evidence carefully using multiple criteria.**

2. **Choose a variety of types of evidence from your available information.**

3. **Make sure you know the source of your evidence and can cite it correctly.**

Evaluate the evidence carefully using multiple criteria.

This is the most important step you take in managing the information you have. You can't include all of the information available on your topic, nor would your audience want to listen for that long! Every presentation involves a selection process to decide what gets included and what gets left out. Speakers have ethical responsibilities to their audiences to be accurate and honest. It is fine to present a particular perspective or to have an opinion about a given topic, but ethically you must still ensure that what you share with your audience is true, reasonably timely, reasonably thorough, and avoids obvious bias.

Evaluating your evidence for **accuracy** is the first criteria you need to apply. This can present some challenges, especially on controversial topics or with a topic about which not much is known. A good place to start is with the source itself. Where did your information come from? Is your source a reputable scholarly journal with peer-reviewed articles, or a well-known source of current news? Within the article, can you determine how the information was created? Did the author conduct their own research, or are they reporting what someone else did? As you are evaluating the information you have, it can help to look for facts or ideas that occur in more than one source. That is certainly not a guarantee, but it can indicate a higher likelihood that the information is accurate.

Assuming that the evidence you have is accurate, you will want to consider its **currency**. Generally, more recent information is most relevant to your audience and will add the most value to your presentation. With the fast pace of information creation and technological innovation, information from even two or three years ago is often obsolete or no longer applicable. If you are talking about a particular time in history or presenting a chronological perspective on your topic, then older information can still be relevant. But even if you were discussing the plays written by Shakespeare or the building of the Egyptian pyramids, it is a good idea to look for the most recent information available. New evidence and information still comes up on older topics, and staying current matters now more than ever before.

As you are assessing the accuracy and currency of your evidence, you should also consider the **relevance**. You could find a terrific piece of evidence, absolutely accurate and just out this week – but if it isn't relevant to your topic and what you want your audience to know, understand, or do, it isn't good for you. It is easy to get distracted by a compelling piece of evidence or an intriguing perspective you had not encountered before. It can happen that a great piece of evidence will make you rethink the approach to your topic or what you want to emphasize in your presentation. Be open to that possibility. However, as you are reviewing the information and looking for high quality evidence, you should stay focused on your topic and your presentation goals. Depending on the time you have to speak, it is likely that you will be unable to include much of the evidence you find. Ask yourself, what will my audience get from hearing or seeing this? How does this support my ideas? Is it clear how this connects to my overall perspective on this topic? If you can answer these questions easily, you're on your way to a solidly supported speech.

Choose a variety of types of evidence from your available information.

Once you have a collection of pieces of evidence, you will want to think about the types of evidence you want to include in your presentation. There are three major types of evidence, and each offers something useful and unique to your presentation. The three types are statistics, examples, and testimony. In your presentation, it is a good idea to include all three types, to create a SET of excellent pieces of evidence within your speech.

Statistics are a powerful type of evidence using numbers to express information. Most statistics express a relationship, although often the relationship is implied rather than explicit. For Example, according to the American Veterinary Medical Association, "36.5% of U.S. households own dogs and 30.4% own cats." (AVMA, 2012). This statistic quantifies the relationship of pet owning households to the total number of households. To put those percentages in more concrete terms, according to the AVMA, approximately one out of every three households in the United States owns at least one pet. Statistics are powerful because they tend to be accepted rather than questioned, and the use of numbers carries a tone of authority and competence. Stephen Colbert coined the term "truthiness" to describe information that feels true whether it is actually true or not. For many audience members, statistics feel true. As a speaker, you also gain credibility and authority when you use statistics effectively. Statistics can make you sound more knowledgeable on your subject. For that reason, it is important to evaluate the statistics you use in your speeches carefully and to explain them clearly to your audience. Statistics are generated from many sources for many reasons, and not all statistics are created equally. As with any piece of potential evidence, you want to make sure the statistics that you use are accurate, current, and relevant. More specifically, make sure the statistic you use actually supports the claim you are making. For example, if your speech is about pet ownership, the statistic about dogs and cats could be useful to help your audience get a sense of how prevalent pet ownership is in the U.S., but it does not say if those pet owners are responsible and care for their pets properly, nor does it account for households with multiple pets. It is up to you to determine if the statistical evidence supports your claim, and to explain the numbers to your audience in a way that makes sense but does not overstate or misrepresent the statistical evidence. Election polls are a good example of statistics that are often misrepresented or not fully explained. A poll will offer statistics such as Candidate A has support from 47% of the voters and Candidate B has support from 51%, and so Candidate B is the leader. But in small print, the same poll will indicate a "margin of error" of plus or minus 4 points. If the gap between the candidates is just four points, and the margin of error is four points – then the poll results are meaningless for determining who is ahead at that moment. Such examples of statistics with serious limitations and shortcomings are all too common. Again, it is up to you to find statistics that support the claims you are making and to explain what those numbers mean to your audience. The credibility and power of statistics can work to your advantage if you handle them well.

Examples are another form of evidence, and probably the most commonly used form. Examples come in three forms: the specific instance, the brief example, and the extended or narrative example. The power of examples is in the way that they help your audience to imagine and connect to your topic. Examples can create vivid images and evoke strong emotions in your audience members. They can act like the 'human interest' stories in the news, providing a connection to the personal experiences of your audience. Specific instances are items on a list, usually given in sets of three. In your pet ownership speech, you might say "The most common pets in the U.S. are dogs, cats, and birds." Those are specific instances. A list gives your audience the chance to identify with some aspect of your speech – while they might not own a dog, they might own a cat or a bird, and the list brings them into the speech and encourages them to continue to listen. Brief examples are short stories, approximately 3 to 5 sentences long. Brief examples connect to our human affinity for stories. Stories build understanding, and a brief example can act as a small window into a new idea or concept. The audience can identify with the story in your brief example, even if the example is of something they have never experienced. The key to effective brief examples is to keep them short, vivid, and clearly related to your topic. For example, for the speech on pet ownership, a brief example could describe a pet wedding. "Rocco and Brie spent $5000 on food, fancy clothes, and themed decorations for their wedding last month. More than fifty of their close friends and family members gathered at Rocco and Brie's house to celebrate. When the groom walked around the room and sniffed all the guests, no one was worried – because Rocco and Brie are dogs." Such a short example paints a vivid verbal picture for your audience, helps them connect to your topic, and yet does not take up a lot of time. Brief examples are points of connection and understanding between you and your audience members. The last type of example is the extended or narrative example. Just as it sounds, extended or narrative examples are longer and more detailed stories. The benefit of an extended example is the amount of detail you can include within the longer story framework. If a topic is particularly complex or difficult to understand, an extended example can be very helpful for your audience. Ronald Reagan, president of the United States from 1980 – 1988, was famous for his effective use of extended narrative examples (Lewis, 1987). However, extended examples also take much more time to deliver properly, and if the example does not go over well with your audience, it can become a long and painful experience. It is also easy to get caught up in the details of a narrative example and miss the point of the story, especially if the example is a personal experience. No matter what type of example you choose, it should be vivid, help your audience connect to your topic, and clearly relate to the ideas and claims you want to make.

Testimony is another form of evidence which offers a unique contribution to your presentation. Testimony is evidence from someone with specific expertise or first-hand experience, and is usually presented as a direct quotation. Carefully chosen testimony can be a powerful form of evidence, as it has both authenticity and authority. A good piece of testimony conveys the authority of the person you are quoting, and the authenticity of being someone's actual words. Testimony is commonly categorized into two major types – expert testimony, and peer or lay testimony. Expert testimony most often comes from a person with recognized professional credentials in their area. The Surgeon-General of the United States or the Director of the Center for Disease Control would both have advanced

medical degrees, perhaps additional credentials in public policy, and extensive experience with the policies and practices related to national health issues. They would be considered experts in public health. Peer or lay testimony comes from a person with significant experience in a particular area, but not necessarily professional credentials or degrees.

Basketball player Stephen Curry would likely be considered an expert on his sport, but he does not have a degree in basketball. His authority comes from his personal experience, and he could offer highly authentic peer testimony. Two key aspects for assessing testimony are the person's qualifications on your topic, and the quality of their words. First, it is important to clearly and briefly explain the qualifications of the person to your audience. You get credit from your audience for the quality of the testimony you use; in a way you are borrowing the credibility of the person you are quoting. Additionally, you have the option to use a direct quotation or to paraphrase the person's words. If you do quote the person, you must be sure that you are absolutely accurate in the quotation – use the exact words, and make every effort to keep the quotation in the correct context. It is just as acceptable to paraphrase the person. Unless the quotation is so good or so striking that you cannot even come close to matching it, often you can convey the same information in your own words. The famous quotation from John F. Kennedy's 1960 inaugural address, "My fellow Americans, ask not what your country can do for you; ask what you can do for your country" is so iconic and so powerful, there is no good way to restate it. Kennedy also spoke about the importance of physical fitness and was a strong proponent of the President's Council on Physical Fitness. During his presidency, Kennedy expanded and promoted the program. His support was a significant factor in the program's success and in recognition of the importance of fitness, especially for school children. In a 1961 speech supporting the program, Kennedy said "Physical fitness is not only one of the most important keys to a healthy body, it is the basis of dynamic and creative intellectual activity." This is a strong quote, but it could be reasonably and effectively paraphrased to "Kennedy viewed physical fitness as an important part of creative and intellectual work as well."

Use quotations when they are so great or so eloquent, you can't possibly say it any better; use paraphrases when the quotation is good, not great, and can be effectively restated.

Make sure you know the source of your evidence and can cite it correctly.

While doing your research, it is important to keep track of the sources of the information. You will need to know the author, the publication name or site, and the date your source was published. If you are using information from a website, you need the URL as well as the date and time you accessed the site. Given the likelihood of a link being taken down or revised, that combination allows reasonably precise identification of your source. Oral citations are often different than the written references given at the end of a paper or in the closing visual aid of a formal presentation. You should always give attribution for any information that you did not create yourself, including images in your visual aids. Bear in mind that the abundance of material available on the Internet or via social media does not mean you can use whatever you find. Many images, website materials and other accessible forms of information are protected by copyright. Even if no copyright is present or asserted, never use anything you find without giving credit to the source. YouTube videos, Vines, tweets, Instagram photos, blogs and Facebook posts are examples of public sources that still require citations for anything you use.

Sometimes this will mean giving the entire formal reference orally, but often you can give the most relevant and necessary information about the source without giving the formal reference. This abbreviated form of citation allows you to speak more naturally and stay in the flow of your presentation. For example, if you are citing an article written by Nicholas Kristof in the New York Times, you might not include the author in your oral citation, but instead say "In a New York Times article from May 21, 2016…." If your topic is relevant and your audience is familiar with Kristof's work as a journalist and advocate, you might want to cite him more directly "In May 2016, Nicholas Kristof's column in the New York Times covered…." Both oral citations will let your audience know that the material came from a credible source and where they could find more information; neither is a complete and formal reference. As noted above, failing to properly cite your sources is plagiarism. See Chapter 2 to reference Camden County College's Academic Honesty Policy as it pertains to plagiarism.

Placing Information

When you have gathered and assessed a substantial collection of possible pieces of evidence, it's time to work through the process of deciding what to use and how to place it in your presentation. You already know that different types of evidence offer different benefits within a presentation. It's also important to consider your audience's abilities to understand and process information. We know that the average rate of speed for a speaker is about 100-175 words per minute, and we know that the average listener can take in about 300 words per minute. But those rates don't factor in the time it takes to understand and evaluate information that is unfamiliar, of high interest, or verbally complex. So here is another gap for you to bridge – the gap between your speech rate and your audience's ability to understand.

One good standard for thinking about how much evidence to include is a concept known as the Magical Number 7, Plus or Minus 2 (Miller, 1956). Miller's concept suggests that most humans are able to manage about seven pieces of information at one time. Here, "manage" means to understand, hold in short term memory, and be able to put in context. In more (or less) challenging situations, or with audiences who are more (or less) capable or interested, the number rises to about 9 or drops to about 5. As a speaker, you can be thoughtful about how much information you give your audience at any one time, and how you can place it within your speech to maximize comprehensibility. This is accomplished in three ways – by limiting how much evidence you include, by "chunking" your information to maximize audience comprehension, and by positioning your strongest evidence for maximum effect.

First, select only the best possible evidence, thereby limiting the total amount of evidence you present. Knowing that each type of evidence offers different benefits, you will want to try to choose what to include based both on the quality of the content and the effect of a given type of evidence. Too much of any one type of evidence can seem unbalanced and sound awkward. For most speeches, choosing a variety of types of evidence to create a SET is an effective approach. Creating a SET for your speech means you have included at least one or two pieces of each type of evidence—Statistics, Examples, and Testimony—in your speech. A more technical speech would likely have more statistics, a speech to share an experience more examples or testimony, but creating a SET gets you off to a good start.

Second, "chunk" your supporting material and evidence into fewer pieces. Using an outline can be very helpful in this process. As you think through your main points, sub-points, and the supporting evidence you want to include, you are already chunking your information. For example, one of your main points could include two subpoints, each with two pieces of supporting evidence. With good verbal cues from you (e.g. "The point of this example is…"), your audience will process the supporting material and evidence and associate them with your main and sub-point. Now your audience is ready and able to take in more of your great information!

Finally, think about each main and sub-point in the body of your speech and what evidence you have that most powerfully and directly supports that respective point. When you use an example or peer testimony, you may want to support it with a statistic to make your case stronger and increase your credibility. Space out the evidence, keeping it balanced among all of your main and sub-points; don't put all of your evidence under just one main point. Remember, your audience can only process and give context to a small bit of information at a time so use your evidence under each main point for the maximum effect.

11

Visual Aids for Effective Communication

Dr. Tracey Quigley Holden

University of Delaware

Wherever we go in this world, our eyes are met with signs and symbols, visual aids that we connect with on a day-to-day basis. Street signs inform us as to where we are going. Billboards try and persuade us to buy an advertised product. Simple symbols let us know where the bathroom is and which receptacle is for trash or recycling. In the world of public speaking, visual aids can be an important part of a presentation, helping to convey your message in a way that can't be achieved through words alone.

Visual aids, when properly used, can be a wonderful addition to any speech. However, it is important to make sure your message is clear before employing them. Be selective about what information you decide to make visible to the audience. Make sure you have a variety of visual aids to illustrate various points in your presentation. Also, be sure you are able to explain and display each visual aid with maximum effect. Finally, when making your presentation, focus your attention on the audience and not the visual aid.

There are two phases when you use visual aids with presentations – development and application. In this chapter, the Five By Five approach will help you through both phases. When you are developing visual aids, there are five rules that will guide you as you create effective visual aids. When you have developed your visual aids and are ready to use them, there are five application principles to guide you so that your message and aids work together to make your presentations as effective as possible. Before we discuss developing and applying visual aids, let's take a look at some common types.

Types of Presentation Aids

Graphs

Advantages: Graphs can render what are complicated figures into visual images that convey statistical information and numerical data in ways an audience can easily understand.

Potential Challenges: Make sure the information conveyed on the graphs is easy to read and easy to explain.

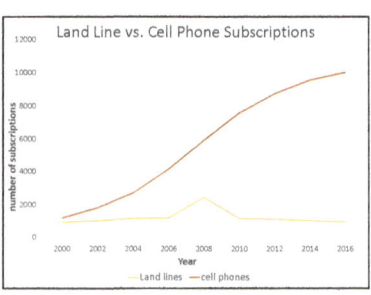

The **line graph** has an x and y axis and a line or lines correlating with statistical information. Such a graph can illustrate the change in sea levels or the decrease in land line telephone usage over time.

Pie graphs are good for representing different slices or segments of information related to a specific topic.

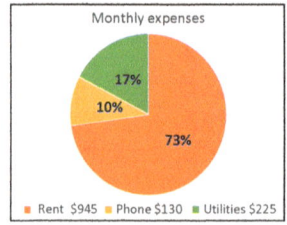

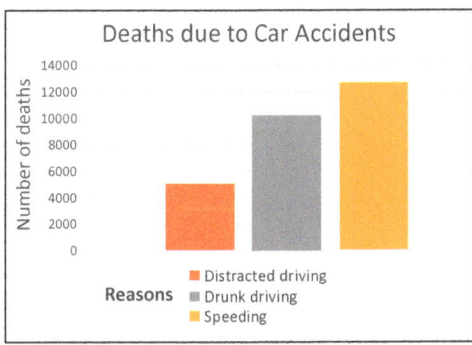

Bar graphs are well suited for comparing and contrasting two or more things.

Charts

Advantages: Like a graph, you can fit a lot of data on a chart. A chart would be a great way to list the largest cities in the world by population or to list the league leaders in a statistical category of a professional sport.

Potential Challenges: Charts are not as visually stimulating as graphs or photographs and can leave less of an impression on the viewer. Also, in creating a chart a presenter can fall prey to including too much information and thus confuse the audience.

Drawings and Photographs

Advantages: What better way to add to a speech about the architect Frank Lloyd Wright than to include sample drawings of his work? Drawings could also come in handy when presenting on archaeological findings from a Mayan temple or Roman tomb. Likewise, a photograph can be useful in conveying the visual power of something like the Golden Gate Bridge when a model or the object itself is unavailable.

Potential Challenges: It is crucial that the drawings and photographs are large enough for the audience to see the subject matter. PowerPoint is an excellent way to show these visual aids during your presentation. If there is text on these images make sure it is legible for the audience.

Presentation Technology

Power Point

Advantages: A program such as PowerPoint can integrate a variety of visual aids into one clean and colorful mode of presentation.

Potential Challenges: Problems can occur when speakers rely too heavily on the program and not the presentation. Technology will not substitute for well-ordered content; it will only enhance it.

Video

Advantages: They say a picture is worth a thousand words. The same can be said of a video. Suppose you were making a speech about hurricanes. Video footage of such storms could really bring the point home about their power and effect on buildings and infrastructure, not to mention the heavy human cost.

Potential Challenges: If the video is too long, poorly edited, or set up improperly it can take away from the speech itself. Poor resolution and other technical issues can be thoroughly distracting and undermine the effectiveness of your presentation. Also, be sure that your video is not too long. It certainly shouldn't be longer than a minute.

Objects

Advantages: Using objects related to your speech can be a great way to shed light on your message and make a powerful impression. A historical speech on mining might call for you to bring in an old pick axe. A speech on how kites are made might warrant bringing in a kite.

Potential Challenges: Sometimes the physical characteristics of an object can make it difficult to use in a presentation. If your object is in any way dangerous it shouldn't be part of your speech. For your presentation on mining it wouldn't be a good idea to bring in a case of dynamite. Similarly, the physical properties of certain objects make using them in a presentation prohibitive. Make sure the object is not too large to transport and not too small so the audience will have to strain to see it. And, do not pass around any items during your speech; it becomes a distraction as the speech progresses.

Developing SMART Visual Aids - Five Rules

Before you begin to develop visual aids for your presentation, make sure your central message, main points, and supporting evidence have been thoroughly prepared. In our visually oriented society, too many speakers make the mistake of starting with the preparation of their visual aids rather than their message. A good visual can inspire a good message, or even be the focus of your content, but the message must come first. In order for your presentation to be effective, your message must be at the center of your presentation. Imagine if your presentation was to introduce a new car. You could have dozens of pictures of the vehicle, engineering graphics of its mechanics, video of the car's performance, and even a model of the car itself, but without a clear and compelling message explaining how the car works and what is new and terrific about its performance and design, the presentation would fall flat. Your visual aids need to be tailored to the information you want your audience to understand. Visual aids can help your audience more readily comprehend complex ideas and increase their interest in your topic, but even the best visual aids cannot deliver your message as effectively as you can. The acronym SMART describes how to prepare visual aids to enhance your presentation. If you choose to use visual aids, you can use these ideas to develop SMART visuals that help your audience and you feel SMART about your topic and the effectiveness of your presentation.

Strong, supportive visual aids are built on five key qualities. Each quality is linked to how humans process information and how speakers are most effective in delivering information.

The first rule is: *simple visual aids are easy for your audience to understand.* Any visual aid you use should be designed so that your audience can see and understand the key concept within 10 to 15 seconds. If you are using a chart or graph, the audience may need a little more time to read all the labels, but the concept being presented should not require more than a quick glance at the graph or chart title. Keep in mind you want your audience to be paying attention to you and your message, and not spending their time trying to understand a complicated visual aid. One basic design concept that helps keep visual aids simple is to think in terms of statement + image. Each visual aid should make (or have as a label) a single statement contributing to your message, and have an accompanying image to demonstrate that statement. Other information may be in the visual aid, but the central idea and image should be immediately apparent to your audience.

The second rule is: *memorable visual aids are striking to the eye;* they present information using strong visual cues and elements to draw the viewer in and highlight important aspects of the information being presented. An easy way to add memorability to your visual aids is to limit the amount of text and add color. Most likely you have been to a presentation where the speaker showed slides with lots of text, and perhaps even read from the slide. This all but defeats the purpose of a visual aid. Showing information you can give verbally is a waste of time and can create boredom and restlessness in your audience. This is especially true of written text! Instead, use an eye-catching visual image with minimal or no text. Color should be used as an accent – too much and your audience gets distracted or overwhelmed. Think about how a good designer will use a neutral color as a base, then add contrasting colors in accessories. The smaller "pops" of color attract attention to those pieces, while at the same time adding depth to the base. Good design, color, and strong images should showcase the features of your visual aid that give your audience insight into your message.

The third rule is: *add information to your presentation.* Good visual aids do more than just present a pretty picture — they provide information to your audience in a way that words are not as efficient at doing. The old saying "a picture is worth a thousand words" is true in many situations, but not for all pictures. If you are trying to explain a complex process or object, a picture or model can convey that information efficiently and effectively. Never show an image or use a visual just for the sake of having a visual. For example, if you are giving a presentation about the harmful effects of poaching on African elephants, it is probably safe to assume your audience knows what an elephant looks like. Showing your audience a picture of an elephant adds no information to your presentation. Creating a graph using elephant icons to show the numbers killed by poachers each year would add information and do so in a visually memorable and effective way.

Along with making sure your images add to your presentation, make sure that you are using images appropriately. Pictures, images, graphs, charts, and other visuals are subject to the rules of plagiarism just as text or any other form of evidence. Many pictures and visuals available on the Internet are copyrighted and you cannot use them without permission and will often have to pay a fee for their use. Sometimes images will have a watermark or copyright imprint on the image to indicate their restricted use. Unless you have created the image yourself, always provide a reference or URL directly on the visual aid to credit your source correctly.

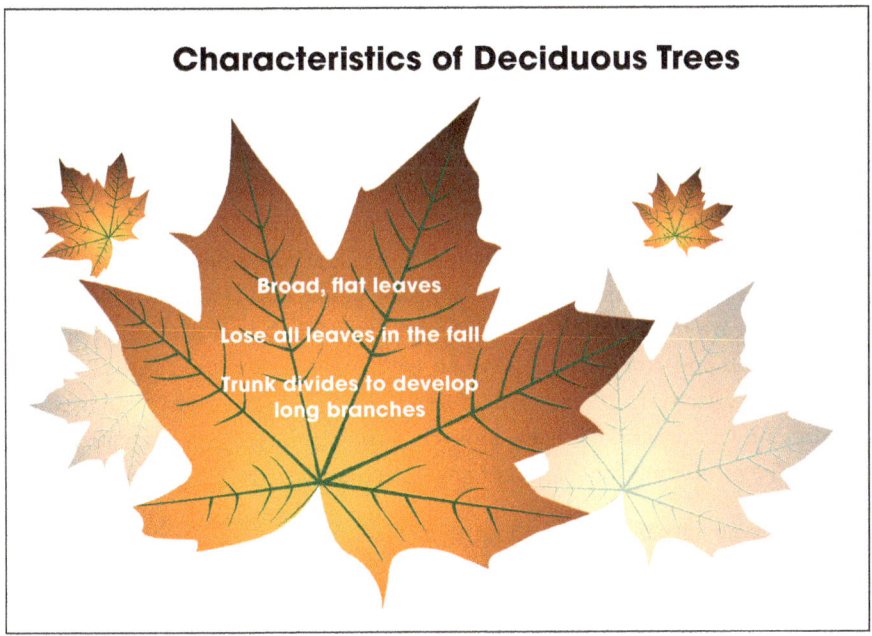

The fourth rule is: *readable text and clearly visible images are a must for any visual aid you use.* The classic elementary school poster with the words bunching up to one side or trailing around the edge should be a warning to you. Generally, your font size for any text should be at least 24 point; the person in the back row of your audience should not have to squint to read your text. Along with being large enough for easy reading, keep the amount of text to a minimum. Too much text on a screen is both distracting and boring to your audience, and tends to increase your likelihood of reading it! A good rule to follow is the 5 x 5 rule — have no more than 5 lines of text on a slide, and no more than 5 words per line. That means you are limited to 25 words per slide. The 5 x 5 rule usually allows you to increase your font size as well, which increases your readability.

Just as your text should be easily readable, any images used should be clear and sharp. Keep in mind that when you project images on to a screen, they quickly become grainy and faded as they expand. Finally, limit the number of images you use. One image and a caption are far more powerful than a collage of small images and small text, or even a group of images. Five images on a screen should be your limit, and those should be carefully placed and sized. Too many images at once quickly become visual clutter, rather than contributing to your audience's understanding.

The fifth rule is: *technology independent.* While the use of technology for visual aids has become almost ubiquitous, your presentation should not depend on technology. You must be prepared for technology to fail, and be able to give your presentation without any visual aids at all. As the character John Bender says in the movie The Breakfast Club (1985), "It's an imperfect world. Screws fall out." Technology fails. Projectors don't connect, links don't work, videos don't load, programs crash, and systems are incompatible or simply not available. No matter what happens, your message and content should be so well prepared that you can give your presentation effectively independent of technology. If you have it in mind that you can present with or without visual aids, you won't be flustered if something goes wrong. The most important aspect of any presentation is delivering the message!

Preparing your visual aids according to the SMART guidelines will help you be ready to present with great visuals. But as mentioned above, you need to use those great visual aids in the most effective way possible. The next section of this chapter will discuss five principles for using visual aids to enhance your presentation and support your message.

Using Visual Aids – The Five Principles

Once you have created your visual aid using the Five Rules, you can make sure you use it most effectively by following the Five Principles. Each principle stands alone, but also works with the other four principles and the Five Rules to help you prepare and deliver your final presentation with poise, confidence, and maximum effect.

The first principle for effective use of visual aids is to *make sure your message is clear before you consider adding visuals.* That means your research, key points and evidence, organization and overall presentation form are all complete. At that point, you are ready to consider what, if any, visual aids would be most useful to your audience. Visual aids are just that – aids to support and facilitate our messages, not replacements of our messages. If we are not clear about our content, about what we want to communicate, visual aids can only clutter the message. If our message is well prepared and clear, good visual aids can help our audiences more readily understand and grasp the meaning and significance of our messages.

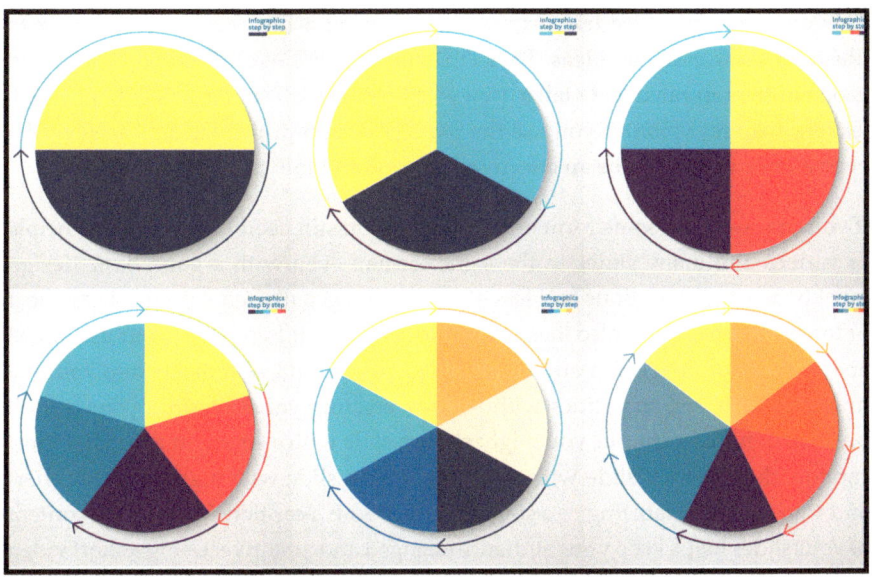

The second principle is to *be selective about visual aids*. For most presentations, a good guideline to follow is to have no more than one or two visual aids per main point. If you have three main points, then that means no more than six visual aids total (screen shifts or views would be the Prezi equivalent). There is some flexibility with this principle. You may have a topic that is highly visually oriented, or need a couple more visual images to help your audience understand a particularly complex concept. But starting with just one or two visual aids, slides, or views per main point will still help you select only the best and most helpful visual support for message and your audience.

The third principle is to *consider a variety of visual aids*. There are almost unlimited possibilities for adding visual interest to your presentation. Although current trends are toward electronic visual aids, there are many other options. An actual example or model of an item you are discussing can be very effective. If you were talking about 3D printing, bringing in a 3D printer, samples of what can be printed, or even demonstrating how to use the printer would be a highly effective visual aid. If you want audience interaction within your presentation, using a blackboard, whiteboard, or even large flip charts on easels to illustrate ideas or record audience responses might be a great visual representation of your core message concepts. Simon Sinek, the ethnographer and leadership expert, gave a terrific TED talk in 2009 on "How great leaders inspire action" using a flip chart and a marker to illustrate a few essential ideas. That TED talk now has over 27 million views and is one of the top rated TED talks. (www.ted.com/talks/simon_sinek_how_great_leaders_inspire_action) If you use the SMART design principles discussed earlier, even a basic poster can be an effective, low-cost and low tech visual aid.

If you choose to use some form of technology, you still need to apply the principle of variety. Too many slides in the same format, even with a good basic design, quickly become repetitive and less effective. Slides with bullet points, heavy text, or too many images are also ineffective. Not only should you limit your use of text and number of images on any single slide, you should also make sure you mix up slides with text and slides with images, creating variety within your overall presentation. For example, you might show a slide with a strong image and a short caption, then another slide with an image, then a slide with a graph or bar chart and some detailed labeling or a single number with a caption. Varying the content of your slides helps keep your audience engaged and attentive. Using a short video can be a very effective visual aid and can add sound to your presentation. Video clips need to be carefully considered – they should be short, on point, and readily available. Downloading the video you plan to use is your best option; depending on access to YouTube or some other site is always a risk.

The fourth principle is *explaining and displaying your visual aids for maximum effect.* If at all possible, you should only show your visual aid when you are talking about it or explaining it to your audience. If you have a model or other physical aid, covering it or turning it around is one solution. If you are using an electronic presentation, it is a good practice to build in blank slides or neutral background views in between those with information or images. The blank slides allow your audience to return their full attention to you and your message. When you do show a visual, it is important to explain how the visual aid connects to your message and any detailed content you want your audience to understand. You should never show something to your audience without commentary, no matter how clear it may seem to you. If you are showing a video, be sure to set up what they are about to watch so your audience understands what they are looking for in the clip. When using graphs or charts, be sure to state the overall purpose of the chart, and then explain the specific details or concepts that are being illustrated. If you have a particularly complex or detailed image, you do not have to explain every label or facet of the visual. Your role as the presenter is to verbally highlight the information related to your message, not to explain every detail of the visual aid. If there is something particularly obvious and striking about a visual, but unrelated to your message, acknowledge that aspect and redirect your audience to the relevant parts of the visual aid.

The fifth principle is simple but often challenging – *don't talk to your visual aid!* You are there to present your message to your audience. Talking to your screen or your poster or your model defeats the purpose of your presentation, and actually disconnects you from your audience. A quick glance at your visual aid as you initially present it, or a guiding look as you actually point to something specific on the visual aid are acceptable, but you should make every effort to keep your eyes and your focus on your audience members. It should be obvious, but reading from your visual aid is an absolute taboo. If you need to read an extended quote or detailed statistic, put them on your notes rather than read from the screen or visual, and only if you believe the information is so powerful it has to be included. Reading to your audience implies that they are unable to do so for themselves – avoid it at all costs.

Conclusion

In this chapter, you have learned Five Rules for developing SMART visual aids and the Five Principles for using visual aids effectively. The Five by Five approach to visual aids keeps your focus on the message you want to give and the audience you want to communicate with. If you keep in mind that your message should always be the first priority of your presentation, the process of preparing and using visual aids will not only be easier, but your visual aids will contribute more to your presentation and your audience's understanding. Visual aids can support and enhance your message and your content, but they cannot replace either your message or you as the presenter.

References

McLuhan, M. and Quentin Fiore. (1967) The Medium is the Massage: An Inventory of Effects. London: Penguin Books.

Sinek, S. (2009) How great leaders inspire action. TED Talk, TEDxPugetSound. www.ted.com/talks/simon_sinek_how_great_leaders_inspire_action

Stokes, D. and Stephen Biggs. (201x) The Dominance of the Visual." Unpublished ms.

12
Using Language

David Pallant
County College of Morris

The ability to appropriately select and adjust your language during the speech is as critical to successful speaking as topic selection, audience analysis, and delivery. Words have enormous influence, and finding the right word that can explain, inform, persuade, or entertain audiences is not always an easy task. If we attempt a semantic analysis of the different American English phrases used to inform someone that an individual has died, we can see that there are a variety of ways to say a similar thing. Semantics is the science or study of the meanings of words, symbols, and language. Insofar as these features of communication are central to effective speaking, a speaker's attention to semantics is essential. Therefore, let us first consider the following semantic properties of our speech: accuracy, clarity, conciseness, and appropriateness of our language.

Semantic Properties of Speech

Accuracy

The language should strive for accuracy during the speech to build trust and credibility. It must be correct — in grammar and word selection -- and truthful in expression. An informative speech that states a statistic incorrectly can lead the audience to question the credibility of the speaker. For example, a speaker who states that the United States has a population of 315 billion people (confusing the term 'million' with 'billion') would confuse the audience. The use of a wrong word can also affect your credibility; people will think you are incompetent. A student once wrote that he "must obtain classes;" the proper word in this context would have been "take," not "obtain." Also, be aware of the inaccuracies of the combinations of words. For example, "pronunciate" is not a word; it is a combination of the words "pronounce" and "enunciate," each word means something different. One error to watch out for is the malapropism – the inadvertent use of a word or a phrase in place of one that sounds like it: the use of "prescription" for "subscription" or "persecuted" for "prosecuted." Such mistakes are liable to make audience members disengage for a presentation.

Clarity

The language of a speech should also strive for clarity. Clear and familiar language allows for proper audience comprehension. For an example of clarity in language we can look at the medical profession. A doctor or EMT may use the term flatlined to infer that the patient's heartbeat has "flatlined" on a heart monitor. The key to being clear is to use concrete language – language that is specific and precise. General words or phrases like "stuff" and "things like that" are vague, thus meanings and interpretations are left up to the imagination of the audience. Using a word like "adolescent" is more specific than the word "child;" both are acceptable, however, by using a specific word you have painted a more detailed picture in your audience's mind. Descriptive adjectives and adverbs will create vivid images, appealing to your listeners' senses. For example, if you were persuading your audience that the roads in your neighborhood needed to be repaved you wouldn't just say "the road is a mess," you would say "when driving over the crumbly, pot-hole filled road, I was bounced around like a ping-pong ball." Be creative with your descriptions. For example, if you're talking about stocks, saying "Delta's stock went up" is boring; "Delta's stock gained altitude" is a clever use of words, and will catch your audience's attention to keep them listening. Using a thesaurus will help you find a word that will create a more vivid context. If you want to get your specific message across, use clear and specific language.

Conciseness

The language of a speech should strive for conciseness. Shorter sentences are more easily processed when listening. Say it as simply as you can; eliminate the word clutter. Using extra words doesn't make you sound smarter; it will make your audience stop listening.

Appropriateness

Lastly, the language of a speech should always be appropriate toward the audience, context, environment, and type of speech. As a general rule it is recommended that speakers avoid jargon, which is the language, especially the vocabulary, peculiar to a particular trade, profession, or group. It would not be appropriate to use the term "Myocardial Infarction" during an informative speech to a general population of students on campus, unless it were defined. However, it might be appropriate to use this term, and presume the audience understands its meaning, when presenting to a group of medical students.

Also, think about the audience's level of knowledge on the topic. Sometimes you can do a pre-speech survey to get this information. You don't want to give information that will go over their heads and you don't want to give too much basic information to sound condescending.

President Truman hired a speechwriter to use "forty-dollar words." Fancy and technical words can go to waste on your audience. Select a level of language that is appropriate for your audience; third graders can understand quantum physics if the vocabulary is at their level and the topic is related to *their* experiences. Astrophysicist Neil deGrasse Tyson broke down the complex topic of astrophysics in his book *Astrophysics for People in a Hurry* (2017) such that a person with no scientific background can understand the topic.

The last thing you want to do is offend anyone in your audience. Be sensitive to cultural differences and use language that is respectful and inclusive. Avoid words that stereotype, demean or patronize people on the basis of age, ethnicity, gender, class, or disability. Non-sexist, or gender-neutral language should be used to show equality of the genders with respect to jobs and social roles.

Now consider the following semantic variations that are called for in different contexts even with regard to the very same event: a person's dying. A speaker, depending on the context, may be trying to inform, or persuade, or entertain, or commemorate. Here are different phrases or words to describe that someone has died. Try to consider which type of speech, and in what setting, it is appropriate to use these phrases. The initial list of phrases below lists euphemisms. A euphemism is the substitution of a mild, indirect, or vague expression for an expression that means the same thing but is thought to be more offensive, harsh, or blunt. If a speaker uses these euphemisms in a persuasive or commemorative speech, it may be a kinder, more subtle way to say that someone has died. The speaker might say that someone

"has passed away,"

"departed,"

"was called home,"

"slipped away,"

"lost his/her battle,"

"left this world,"

In contrast to euphemisms, the following phrases are more technical and direct. A speaker might use these terms in an informative speech, especially if it were a more technical context. It would be appropriate to use these phrases to present a speech topic that concerns the medical profession or law enforcement. Someone

"has expired,"

"is deceased,"

"has terminated,"

"has flatlined,"

There are also dysphemisms. A dysphemism is the substitution of a harsh, disparaging, or unpleasant expression for a more neutral one. These could be used effectively during an entertainment or commemorative speech if the context is appropriate and the appropriate degree of respect is maintained for the audience and subject of the speech. Someone

"has kicked the bucket"

"met one's maker,"

"has croaked,"

"is pushing up daisies,"

Informative speeches need to use non-judgmental language and always eliminate the personal perspective. A speaker should not pick a side, profess an opinion, or insert a judgment during an informative speech. The informative speech is meant to teach, clarify, or define a topic for an audience. The point of this sort of presentation is for the audience to learn, to expand their knowledge, and to have a deeper understanding of the topic after an informative speech. Thus the following phrases would have no place in an informative speech: "I believe," "I know," "In my experience," "In my opinion." More appropriate phrases would be phrases such as, "The research states," "According to…," and "Experts on the matter have said." These sorts of phrases are suggested for the informative speech. Audiences are sensitive to the use of pronouns (I, we, you, us, our, them, and they) in your speech. Informative speech relies mainly on referencing credible, authoritative, third-party sources, when references are used. The speaker is typically not such a referential source but rather a source of information about what the experts are saying. The speaker's pronoun use should, naturally, reflect that.

A persuasive speech should use these pronouns to evoke and provoke an audience to the perspective and position of the speaker. For example, the use of "You have the power to change this country," or "We have the power to change this country," or "The power to change this country is in your hands, not mine." These expressions are inclusive. (They use first and second person pronoun references.) The use of language is not informative, in the sense we've described, but rather it is designed to stir certain emotions and evoke certain thoughts to which the speaker would like the audience to become or remain strongly committed, that is to say, to be persuaded.

A commemorative (e.g. eulogy or wedding), entertainment, or narrative speech should employ effective story telling techniques. Usually the purpose of these types of speeches is to tell a story about a person, topic, or organization. The speaker should present a logical summary of someone's life, pay tribute, or provide the audience with a moral or value lesson. At some point in your life you will probably be asked to prepare, practice, and perform this type of speech. Please remember that these types of speeches can have an enormous effect on an audience, and the speaker has power and responsibility over the audience. These types of speeches can even result in a degree of personal empowerment for the speaker.

Rhetorical Devices

Now that you know you need clarity in your language and that being concise and appropriate is of the utmost importance, we need to spice up your speech to stimulate the senses of your audience. We can do this by using rhetorical devices, also known as Stylistic or Speech Devices. They can be placed into two categories: imagery and rhythm.

Imagery includes simile, metaphor, analogy, and personification.

Simile — explicitly compares one thing to another, using "like" or "as" to do so. If you were giving an informative speech on life's challenges you could open your speech with "Life is like a roller coaster."

Metaphor — also compares two things, but does so by representing one thing as actually being the other. It makes an implicit, implied, or hidden comparison between two things that are unrelated, but which share some common characteristics. To change the above simile to a metaphor omit the word 'like' – "Life is a roller coaster." If you are doing a persuasive speech on convincing your school district to get new computers you could say "the computers we have are dinosaurs."

Analogy — an extended metaphor or simile that compares an unfamiliar concept or process to a more familiar one to help listeners understand the unfamiliar one. If you are giving a speech on Boeing's new 777 that has a maximum fuel capacity of 31,000 U.S. gallons, and you want your audience to understand how much fuel that really is, you can compare it to how many times their bathtub has to be filled to the brim to equal 31,000 gallons (the answer – 1,292; that's filling it every day for three and a half years).

Personification – giving human traits or qualities to inanimate objects, animals, or ideas. When giving an informative speech about the seasons each main point could be worded as a personification of the season, for example "Old Man Winter is fierce," "Spring announces the rebirth of nature," "The summer drowns us in sunshine," "Autumn tosses the leaves to the ground."

Rhythm – includes parallelism, repetition, alliteration, and antithesis.

Parallelism – a similar arrangement or pattern of words that is duplicated. It is used to emphasize relationships. You can use parallel structure to introduce main points (see examples of main points in Chapter 4) or to emphasize sub-points in the speech. Here's an example of using parallel structure to introduce main points from Steve Jobs' Stanford Commencement Address:

It means to try to tell your kids everything you thought you'd have the next 10 years to tell them in just a few months. **It means to make** sure everything is buttoned up so that it will be as easy as possible for your family. **It means to say** your goodbyes.

Repetition – the restating of a word or phrase to add emphasis to ideas. The above example is also an example of repetition.

Alliteration – saying the same sound in a sustained sequence. If you want to convince your town council to have lunch hour concerts in your local church you might phrase it like this: "Trade cell phones for Chopin and Blackberries for Bach." Or, if there was a major national disaster you might say that "the Red Cross was brought out to counsel the confused in Columbus, help the heartbroken in Hartford, support the saddened in Sacramento."

Antithesis – the juxtaposition of contrasting ideas, usually in parallel structure. The most common example of this is John F. Kennedy's "Ask not what your country can do for you; ask what you can do for your country." If you were doing a speech about the moon landings you might use Neil Armstrong's quote "That's one small step for a man, one giant leap for mankind."

13

Preparing for Speech Delivery

Dr. Sandra French
Radford University

Polishing the Preparation Outline

Once the preparation outline is written, use it to gauge whether your speech successfully meets the criteria of the assignment. Read through your preparation outline as if you were delivering your speech. Is it too long? Too short? Take note of how long it takes you to read through each main point. Are the main points out of balance? Remember that you want to keep each main point within a similar time frame so that your points are balanced and symmetrical.

Remember from Chapter 8, The Preparation Outline, to read through your preparation outline several times. Again, focus on the following:

- Are my main points clear?

  - If you read through your preparation outline for a friend, and if they cannot easily pick out the main points and repeat them back to you, then rephrase them so as to better emphasize them. Repetition of main ideas is the key to their standing out and being grasped and retained by an audience.

- Are my supporting materials clear and supported?

  - Do I have at least one source to support each main point?

  - Am I orally citing my sources?

- Do I have 5 Elements of a Good Introduction?

    - Does my opening serve to capture the attention of my audience?

    - Do I have one sentence explaining the main idea of my speech?

    - Do I establish the relevance of my topic to my audience?

    - Do I establish credibility with the audience?

    - Do I clearly preview the main points to be covered in my speech?

- Do I have transitions that move my audience from the introduction to the speech body, from main point to main point, and from the body into the conclusion?

- Do I have 2 Elements of a Good Conclusion?

    - Have I effectively and succinctly signaled to the audience that my speech is ending?

    - Have I restated my Central Idea?

    - Lastly, is there a strong finish to my speech?

While your individual speaking assignments will vary, most preparation outlines should include these components. See below for a full length example of a preparation (full sentence) outline.

SAMPLE PREPARATION OUTLINE
with labels

Topic: Strokes

Specific Purpose Statement: To inform my audience about strokes

Central Idea: There are two different types of strokes and you can identify both of them by the four warning signs.

Title: Time Loss is Brain Loss – The Dangers of Strokes

Introduction

I. Attention getter

   Story

   The scariest day of my life was April 12, 2012, when my grandfather had stroke and almost died.

   Startling statistic

   Each year, approximately 795,000 people suffer a stroke. About 20% of these stroke victims die according to the website StrokeCenter.org.

II. Reveal topic

   Today I am going to inform you about strokes.

III. Relate topic to audience (WIIFM)

   Eighty three percent of strokes occur in individuals over 59 years of age. We all have a grandparent or even a parent that age. Being aware of what's going on during a stroke may be the difference between having that person live and be in our lives longer, or dying.

IV. Establish my credibility

   After my grandfather had the stroke, I did some research to better understand what a stroke is.

V. Preview speech

   Today I will share with you the different types of strokes, as well as how to recognize the warning signs.

Transition: Let me begin with the two main types of strokes.

Body

I. There are two types of strokes.

    A. Hemorrhagic is the rarer of the two main types of stroke.

        1.   An intracerebal hemorrhage occurs due to the rupturing of weakened blood vessels in the brain.

           a. Blood then leaks into surrounding brain tissue.

           b. The bleeding causes brain cells to die and the affected part of the brain stops working correctly.

        2.   A subarachnoid hemorrhage involves bleeding in the area between the brain and the tissue covering the brain.

           a. It is most often caused by a burst aneurysm.

           b. It can also be caused by bleeding disorders, head injury, or blood thinners.

    B. Ischemic strokes are more common.

        1.   According to the website strokeinfo.org, 87% of all strokes are ischemic.

        2.   Ischemic strokes occur when blood vessels become blocked, often by a blood clot.

           a. Blood clots can form due to vessels being clogged with fat and cholesterol.

           b. The blockage keeps blood from reaching the brain, depriving it of oxygen and key nutrients.

Transition: Now that you know about the two main types of strokes, let's discuss the four major warning signs.

  II. To remember the four warning signs of stroke, the Stroke Association encourages people to remember the acronym FAST.

A. The "F" stands for face drooping, where one side of the face droops or is numb.

    1. To check this symptom, simply ask the person to smile.

    2. Observe their smile to see if it is uneven or lopsided.

B. The "A" stands for arm weakness.

    1. Often a person having a stroke cannot lift both arms evenly.

      a. Ask the person to raise both their arms.

      b. Watch to see if one arm drifts downward.

    2. Sometimes one or the other arm can become numb.

C. The "S" stands for speech difficulty or slurred speech.

    1. Ask the person to repeat a simple sentence such as "Ocean water is blue."

    2. Listen for words being mixed up or slurred speech.

D. The "T" stands for time.

    1. This is the most crucial point of all because "time loss equals brain loss" according to the Nittany Valley Rehabilitation Hospital.

    2. If any of these symptoms appear, it is recommended by the Stroke Association that you call 911 immediately, even if the symptoms subside.

Conclusion

    I. Signal ending (and repeating topic is optional)
      In closing, you are now better informed about strokes.

    II. Reinforce the main points/summarize the main points
      Remember that there are two main types of strokes – hemorrhagic and
      ischemic – and four warning signs that are easily remembered with the
      FAST acronym.

    III. Return to story from Introduction
      April 12, 2012, was the worst day of my life due to my grandfather's
      stroke, but Mom's ability to quickly recognize the symptoms and call
      911 saved his life.

Invest the time in creating and polishing the preparation outline. Outlining helps speakers craft more organized, more concise, more memorable messages. By utilizing a preparation outline speakers better learn their material and develop a rhythm and flow in their speaking. As you move from the presentation outline to the speaking outline, you can be more confident in your presentation of the material. This will help you be a more competent speaker.

Converting the Preparation Outline into the Speaking Outline

Once you've practiced your preparation outline in front of a live audience several times and received their feedback on the clarity and power of your message, then you are ready to transfer from your preparation outline to your speaking outline. Many speakers try to skip this step, opting to use their full-sentence outline to deliver a speech. Suffice it to say, this is a mistake. Practicing from a full-sentence outline without utilizing a speaking outline leads to a memorized or partially memorized speech. Delivering one's speech with this lesser preparation offers the speaker no wiggle room. The pressure is on to deliver the speech exactly as it is written on the outline — word for word. The result is a speech that can appear disingenuous. The audience may perceive the speaker's delivery as "wooden." By creating a speaking outline, you can add and include phrases and abbreviations to help you remember key points. You should also add and include things like cues for when to smile or where to pause for dramatic effect.

Transfer the Visual Framework onto the Speaking Notes

Your speaking outline should follow the same visual framework as your preparation outline; it should follow the same visual format with labels, symbols and indentation (see Chapter 8 - The Preparation Outline). Having continuity of framework will make it easier to remember your preparation outline and recall your key points and how to make them.

Figure 13.1 **Key Elements of a Speaking Outline**

1. **Replaces full sentences with phrases and key words**

2. **Forces you to know the material and allows you the freedom to react to the audience and circumstance**

3. **Briefer format allows for more manageable notes**

4. **Helps you to cement the ideas of the speech in their proper order in your memory**

5. **Includes reminders and cues to help your delivery flow smoothly**

Choosing Key Words

The speaking outline uses key words and brief phrases to prompt you through your materials. This forces you as a speaker to really know your material. You internalize your speech rather than relying nearly completely upon an external manuscript or full-sentence outline. One crucial benefit of speaking from a speaking outline, rather than a full-sentence preparation outline, is the freedom it affords a speaker. By using a speaking outline you are free to actually respond to audience feedback and adjust to their message, rather than blindly delivering a fully pre-scripted performance. You have more freedom to speak extemporaneously when it is helpful to do so.

A second benefit is that a speaking outline is much briefer and can easily be put on index cards or printed on paper, as determined by the speaking situation and/ or assignment requirements. You should still write out any quotations in full to ensure that you deliver them accurately, and often speakers will still include the introduction and conclusion in full-sentences to help ensure the presentation starts and ends smoothly. Whether you choose index cards or 8½ x 11 inch sheets of paper, be sure to number them. Speakers who fail to heed this advice often find out the hard way that they should have followed it. I encourage all my students to follow this rule. One speaker, a Big 10 football player with a serious case of nerves, failed to heed my advice. While speaking his hands began shaking violently resulting in his index cards falling to the floor in a scattered heap. Failure to number his cards caused him to lose his place and only regain it after what seemed an eternity, both to himself and to his audience. Remember that even numbered index cards can get disorganized if you shuffle them in your hands. When using a speaking outline on index cards, either place your cards on the lectern (if you have one), or practice holding them in one hand only so your other hand can freely gesture as appropriate. When using 8½ x 11 inch sheets of paper place them side by side on the lectern so either, or both hands can be used for gesturing.

Whether you use a full sheet of paper or index cards, you should practice with your speaking outline so that you feel comfortable with a quick look at your speaking outline to prompt your next speech point. Another benefit to creating a speaking outline is that as you work on the conversion of the preparation outline into the speaking outline you will naturally begin to learn the ideas of the speech in order. Repetition breeds familiarity. By practicing and by converting your preparation outline to a speaking outline, you will be cementing your speech order in your memory.

Choose Cues for the Vocal and Physical Performance

A final benefit of using key words and brief phrases in the speaking outline is that it frees up space on the page for other directions you want to remember. Using a different font color in the margins, provide yourself key reminders such as "pause here for a count of three," "look up," or "smile!" It can be difficult, particularly for novice speakers, to keep these things in mind when presenting. These reminders serve an important role in seamlessly weaving together the components of speech structure, speech content, and speech delivery.

SAMPLE SPEAKING OUTLINE

Introduction

    I. April 12, 2012

    II. Today I'm going to inform you about strokes. EYE CONTACT

    III. 83% strokes over 59 years old
        Grandparent or parent that age
        Being aware can be the difference
        between living or dying.

    IV. I did some research to better understand.

    V. Today I will share with you the types of strokes, as well as how to recognize the warning signs.
        PAUSE HERE

Transition: Let me begin with the two main types of strokes.

Body

    I. Two types of strokes

      A. Hemorrhagic - rarer

        1. An intracerebal hemorrhage – rupturing of weakened blood vessels
          SHOW VISUAL AID
          a. Blood leaks
          b. Brain cells to die

        2. A subarachnoid hemorrhage – bleeding between brain and the tissue
          a. often caused by a burst aneurysm
          b. also by bleeding disorders, head injury, or blood thinners

B. Ischemic — more common

    1. strokeinfo.org. — 87% of all strokes are ischemic.

    2. Blood vessels blocked — blood clots. SHOW VISUAL AID
       a. Clogged with fat and cholesterol.
       b. Deprives brain of oxygen and key nutrients.

Transition: Now that you know about the two main types of strokes, let's discuss the four major warning signs.

II. The Stroke Association — the acronym FAST.

    A. Face drooping.
       1. Check person's smile

       2. Observe if lopsided

    B. Arm weakness.
       1. Cannot lift both arms evenly.

         a. Raise both arms

         b. Watch arm drifts downward
           DEMONSTRATE

       2. Numbness in either arm

    C. Speech problems.
       1. Repeat "Ocean water is blue"

       2. Listen – words mixed up or slurred speech

    D. Time.
       1. "Time loss equals brain loss" according to the Nittany Valley Rehabilitation Hospital

       2. Call 911 immediately if symptoms appear, recommended by the Stroke Association

Conclusion

    I. In closing, better informed about strokes

    II. Two main types of strokes – hemorrhagic and ischemic – and four warning signs FAST

    III. April 12, 2012, worst day – my grandfather's stroke, Mom recognized the symptoms, called 911

Rehearsal and Delivery

You've done your research, written your outline, figured out what you want to say and prepared your presentation aids. There's only one thing left to do and that's deliver your speech. This section will guide you through the important techniques involved in doing just that as well as highlight key strategies for rehearsing your presentation.

When you make your speech be aware of how you use your body. Movement can work to your advantage and appropriate gestures can help augment a speech. However, too much movement can serve to distract an audience and signal nervousness that can diminish a speaker's credibility.

Eye contact with the audience is also important if you want your message to connect. The way in which you use your voice can have a great impact on how the audience receives your message. You should be aware of vocal qualities such as pitch, tone, rate, volume, fluency, and articulation when speaking.

Read on for details regarding these important points concerning the delivery of your speech. At the end of the chapter there is a step-by-step guide for effectively rehearsing your speech.

For many speakers, preparing their speeches — topic selection, research, organization, creating visual aids — is the easiest part of their presentation. When it comes to the actual physical delivery of their message, a new set of issues comes into play. This new set of issues has its own set of challenges and solutions to coordinate and manage. Unlike the earlier preparations, preparing to deliver your speech is all about you and your physical presence as you share the information you've so carefully put together. The good news is that you can prepare for and practice your physical delivery so that how you present your speech actually improves it, helps your audience understand your message, and increases your confidence as a speaker. However, it takes thoughtful practice to get there. In this chapter, we will discuss how your physical and vocal presence and delivery can be practiced to support and even enhance your presentation (Anderson, 2016)(Cuddy, 2017).

Practicing to Deliver Your Speech

In this section, we will discuss the entire process of delivering a speech. The focus here is on physical delivery, so it is assumed that all of your content preparation and organization is done, i.e. that you have already done all your "pre-rehearsal" preparation including the preparation of presentation aids.

First, keep in mind that your presentation begins well before you take your place in front of your audience. Take a minute to recall the material on communication apprehension, commonly called speech anxiety or stage fright. As you get ready to approach your audience, a few deep breaths will reduce any tension you feel. Check your presentation aids – visuals, sound if you're using it, notes – before you move to your primary speaking position. Once you are in front of your audience, hold yourself as tall as you can, with your feet about shoulder width apart. Take a moment to look across all of your listeners, and take one more deep breath. You're ready!

The Physical Presentation

Eye Contact

The eyes have been called the "windows of the soul" and for good reason; we pay a lot of attention to when, how, and what kind of looks people give us. It's important to remember that there are significant cultural differences in what constitutes appropriate and effective eye contact, and we're primarily considering public speaking from a North American perspective. In that context, looking directly at your listeners, and making an effort to include everyone in your audience, is considered the most effective and personable form of eye contact. Looking someone in the eye is associated with trustworthiness, truthfulness, and positivity; looking away, or at the floor, or up in the air is associated with lying, uncertainty, and lack of knowledge. Good eye contact from a speaker means spreading eye contact across the entire audience, pausing to look directly at individuals for a second or two before moving on. Human beings are visually oriented; we want both to see and be seen by others. Making brief eye contact with members of your audience builds on that innate human orientation and at some level fulfills our desire to be acknowledged.

"At least he made eye contact this time."

You may have been told to look just above your audience's heads but not directly in their eyes. This is not recommended. It is an old theater technique called 'cheating the house,' and it only works with very large audiences who can't actually see exactly where you are looking. As a speaker, you want to connect with your audience, not avoid them. At the same time, you don't want to focus on one person or one section of your audience to the extent that others feel excluded. We tend to have a dominant side, usually the same as your preferred hand for writing, and will naturally spend more time looking to that side. Just like crossing a street, look both ways and directly in front of you.

So visually scan the entire audience before you begin speaking. As you speak, move your gaze back across the audience, stopping now and then to look directly at one person or a section of the room. Those stops in your gaze and moments of direct eye contact should last about two or three seconds. Then, move on to the next engagement. Again, your goal is to include everyone in your audience by letting them know you've seen them and appreciate their attention.

Looking at the floor, the ceiling, or at your speaking notes will disconnect you from your audience. Speakers who are trying to remember something – like their memorized speech—will often look up and away from the audience, or at the floor, searching for the missing words. Either one conveys a lack of knowledge and confidence. It's okay to glance at your notes for a second or two, but not much more than that. It's also acceptable to glance briefly at your screen or your presentation aid, but you should not look at them for long. Don't be one of those speakers who reads from their visual aids or explains them at length with their backs turned to the audience. Steady eye contact with your audience will keep them comfortable and engaged with the content you are presenting.

Posture

Standing up straight conveys to the audience that you are both credible and confident in presenting your topic. Hunching over or keeping your head down diminishes your effectiveness in engaging your listeners. However, don't let your body mistake rigidity for good posture. Be comfortable and hold your body in a natural yet poised way.

Motivated Movement

One of the most frequently asked questions from speakers is "Can I move?" The easy answer is "Yes, you can and probably should!" However, there's more to the story.

First, movement is not required, and too much movement can be detrimental to your speech. We have all seen speakers who fidget constantly, or pace back and forth, or just can't seem to stop moving. A lot of random movement is generated by the energy in your body needing somewhere to go, and if you don't direct it, it shows up as a distraction. Human biology demands that we track any type of movement, a throwback to our days as predators or prey. So when you are moving your audience has to pay attention to your movement – and that reduces their ability to pay attention to your message. Avoiding unnecessary and random movement will improve your presentation significantly. Second, you might think if moving is distracting, should I just stand still? That is certainly an option, but standing still reduces your connection with your audience. In many speaking situations, it can be difficult to move in the most effective ways. If you are speaking from a lectern or podium, or if movement might block your presentation aid too much, you may have to stay in place. Standing still won't necessarily reduce your overall effectiveness as a speaker, but if you must or choose to stand still, do your best to connect with your audience as directly as possible using voice technique, eye contact, and gestures. Assuming you can move and do not have to remain in place, there are two fundamental principles for effective movement while speaking. They are: Move only 2 or 3 steps and STOP; and Move with intent.

Figure 13.2 **Fundamental Principles for Effective Movement**

1. Move only 2 or 3 steps and STOP.

2. Move with intent.

The space you have in front of an audience is usually somewhat limited. Even on a relatively large stage, moving too far to one side or the other decreases your ability to connect with audience members on the other side. The other issue is keeping your audience engaged with your message. Knowing that movement is distracting, and yet can add energy and dynamism to your speech, use it sparingly and in small doses. Taking two or three steps and then stopping strikes the right balance.

The timing of your movement matters as well. Of course you can take your two steps at any point during your speech, but there are ways to make the movement work for you. Ideally, your moves come at the same time the speech 'moves' — on transitions between your main points or ideas. Imagine you've spent a few minutes speaking about an important idea, provided several pieces of evidence, and drawn a conclusion about that material. Now you want to tell your audience how the information applies to a current issue. As you give your transition comments, take those two steps. Then *stop* before you begin speaking about the next idea. That small movement signals your audience that something new is being introduced, gives them time to process the last bit of information you delivered, and adds dynamism to your overall delivery. When you *stop*, you signal that they need to pay attention again, you reduce the level of distraction, and give yourself a moment to focus on your next words.

> **Bonus Material. Whenever you give directions or instructions, always stand still. If your audience needs to be able to follow a process step by step, you need to stop while you give them the steps!**

With that in mind, the key to truly polished and effective movement is moving with intent. Just taking a couple of steps in random directions, even if done on transitions, won't add the kind of positive energy you want to create. Additionally, the manner in which you move can contribute to how you feel during delivery and how your audiences perceive you. Moving with intent — firmly taking a step or two to address a new section of the audience, to direct attention to a presentation aid, or to re-center yourself in the speaking space — contributes to your overall presence as a speaker. So before you speak, think through your presentation and consider, when should I move?

Last but not least, there are some types of movement that should be avoided. Pacing back and forth, especially if repeated several times, will only make your audience think of zoo animals. Stepping up and back or side to side, rocking back and forth, twisting on your feet, kicking your feet, tapping your heels or toes, bouncing up and down, leaning on a lectern, table, or chalk board, or the classic wrapping one foot around the other flamingo style won't help you or your audience with your message. So, take your two steps, move with intent, and *stop*.

Gestures

It's possible that the most frequently asked question from speakers is "What do I do with my hands?" Like your body, you can use your hands to support and enhance your presentation. Also like your body, using your hands poorly can distract your audience from your message and even contradict what you're trying to say. Imagine you run into a friend who you know just went through a difficult experience. You say, "Hi, how are you? Everything okay?" and they say "Yeah, fine." However, when they say that, their arms are wrapped tightly around their body, their head is down, and they barely look at you. Is everything fine? No. Their non-verbal communication, and especially the tightly wrapped arms, tells you that things are not fine for them at that moment. The gesture — or in this case the lack thereof — contradicts their words. On the other hand, if they had waved to you as you approached, and in response to your question said "Yeah, fine!" with a dismissive wave of the hand, a strong voice, and looked you in the eye, you would probably think they were doing fine. Their gestures effectively reinforce the message of their words.

One of the amazing things about the human body is how well it is designed to do all the things we want it to do. Consider your arms and hands. Your arm hangs down from your shoulder and bends nicely at the elbow a little above your waist. Your hands can move, point, and rotate on your wrists. All of this happens just underneath your face and your mouth, where your main message is coming from. Although you can't literally talk with your hands in the sense of producing sound, your arms and hands do create a second, powerful line of communication between you and your audience. Using your hands to gesture can reinforce, enliven, and enhance your message. So back to the question – what do you do with your hands? First, keep them between your shoulders and your hips. Old speaking textbooks and speaking coaches used to say to "let your hands hang naturally at your sides," unfortunately, this position doesn't look or feel natural, and it certainly doesn't add to your speech.

Nor should your hands be above your shoulders, unless you're doing a cheer or discussing the wonders of aviation or outer space. The idea is to keep your second line of communication in a supporting role and place. With your hands between your shoulders and hips and arms bent at approximately a 90° angle, you are able to use them most effectively. If you are using notecards, they should be in one hand at a time. If you need to change hands, make sure you complete the pass to your other hand. Notecards should be kept relatively low, so you can glance at them as needed. It's easy but ineffective to wind up with your note cards clasped in both hands, creeping up towards your face like a tiny shield.

Whether you use notecards or not, you can use your hands to reinforce and support your message. It can be helpful to hold up a few fingers as you explain that there are 3 additional points, or 2 compelling ideas. Moving your hands together, palms facing each other, indicates compressing or shortening something, while slicing your hand through the air horizontally can indicate emphasis. An open, upturned palm helps invite your audience into your message, and when you sweep your arms wide with upturned hands, you're inviting everyone into the communicative moment.

There are many powerful and useful gestures, so think about what you're trying to share with your audience and what is most significant about any given part of your speech. Sometimes cueing what is to come is most helpful. At other points conveying emotion or building a connection is more important. As you prepare and practice your speech, mentally note where it feels natural to gesture, and what those gestures do for your message. Good gestures add to your speech, reinforce your message, and help your audience understand your words and your meaning.

An analysis of TED talks (Van Edwards, 2015) shows the most popular TED speakers use the most gestures. In some cases, that's over 600 gestures in just 18 minutes. But like movement, too much gesturing without purpose, especially the same gesture, can distract your audience from your message. Most of us have preferred gestures that we use more frequently than others. President Barack Obama often used an open hand with slightly pointed or pinched together fingers to signify an important idea, sometimes followed with a thump on the lectern for emphasis.

You can probably think of other public figures with distinctive gestures. When a speaker repeats a gesture over and over, the audience can start to watch the gesture rather than listening to the speaker. These repeated hand movements are called *frozen gestures* and should be avoided. Gestures that are more fidgety than meaningful should be avoided as well, since they tend to convey tension and uncertainty. Don't slide charms on a necklace or bracelet, touch your face, twirl or flip your hair, or jingle change in your pocket. Your hands should not be in your pockets during your speech at all. Neither the fig leaf nor drill sergeant (sometimes called "handcuff") hand positions inspire audience confidence; so avoid both. Your gestures should invite your audience into your speech, not shut them out!

Appearance

When speaking in a professional environment, you should have a professional appearance. For gentlemen, that means a button-down shirt and slacks with dress shoes. For women, skirts should be of appropriate length and blouses should not be too form fitting. Comporting yourself in a professional manner throughout your speech or presentation is also paramount to being a well-respected speaker. Credibility comes, in part, from following societal norms so far as what is acceptable dress and decorum.

The Vocal Presentation

Now that you've got a clearer idea about how your body can help you deliver your speech, it's time to consider the instrument carrying your message – your voice. There are six qualities to your speaking voice, and five of them are within your control. **Pitch, tone, rate, volume, fluency, and articulation** each contribute to how your audience hears your message.

The **pitch** of your voice is where you have the least control. The sound of your voice moves across a range of sound, and pitches are the points where a specific sound is heard. You can't control your range, but you can pitch your voice within that range, at least briefly. **Tone** is the quality of the sound as we hear it. Singers and speakers can have great pitch, but still have bad tone. We tend to associate lower, fuller tones with authority and confidence. **Rate** is how quickly we speak, while **volume** is how loudly or softly our voices sound. **Fluency** is our ability to speak without hesitation or **verbal fillers** – those sounds we make when we don't have the words, such as 'um,' 'uh,' and 'like'. Fluency also relates to **pauses**, those moments when we stop talking. **Articulation** is our ability to form sounds clearly and cleanly. Articulation is distinguished from **pronunciation**, which is making the right sounds within a given word. "Nuclear" is pronounced "noo-klee-er," not "nu-cul-your."

Your voice is an incredibly nimble and powerful instrument, and we often fail to take full advantage of how it can enhance speeches. It is worth remembering in this context that for you to speak, you have to breathe first. At the beginning of this chapter, we discussed taking a couple of deep breaths before you start your speech. While it is beyond the scope of this book to detail all the nuances of breath control, you can certainly practice breathing deeply and controlling your breath as you speak. Take a few minutes to breathe in completely, feeling your body fill with air. Then breathe out slowly. You're aiming to breathe out twice as slowly as you breathed in, to control the exit of the air. Do five or ten practice breaths and see how you feel. We tend to breathe rapidly and shallowly when we feel stress, so reminding yourself to breathe deeply (and then doing it) will both help you feel calm and focused and support high vocal quality.

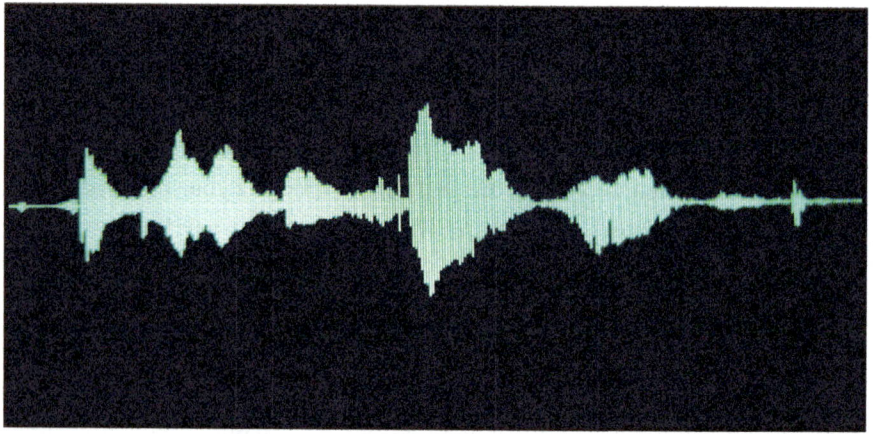

Creating a Dynamic Vocal Variety

When you are ready to give your speech, start by taking at least one or two of those deep, controlled breaths. With your **vocal quality** adequately supported, you will be able to use your optimum pitch and achieve a rich vocal tone. You'll sound great so you can focus on adding vocal variety to your speech to engage your audience. Vocal variety refers to choices you make throughout your speech with all of the vocal qualities. How quickly you speak, when you pause, where you add emphasis, whether you raise or lower your pitch—each aspect contributes to effective communication with your audience. You want your voice to enhance your speech and keep your audience listening. Speaking in a **monotone** – staying on the same pitch, with little variation in rate or emphasis dulls your voice and bores your audience. It's about as far from an engaging conversational tone as you can get. (Word of warning: A monotone sound is much more likely to happen if you try to read your speech word for word.)

Looking back at the vocal qualities, what's optimal for most speaking situations? We have discussed avoiding a monotone already. The kind of vocal variety you're aiming for will vary depending on the speaking situation and topic. It would be appropriate to speak slowly, with a lower **pitch** and restrained **tone**, if you're speaking about a serious topic. For a topic that is more light-hearted, you can speak a bit more quickly with a higher pitch and lively tone. We tend to associate authority and competence with lower pitches and deeper tones, regardless of the gender of the speaker. (Klofstad, 2012) As a general rule, it is better to slow your **rate** when you speak, regardless of the topic. Speaking just a little more slowly than you usually do allows you time to breathe and maintain high vocal quality, and it gives your audience time they may need to hear and comprehend your message. It also helps you to **articulate** your words and make sure your **pronunciation** is correct. There are regional differences in articulation, such as the dropping of 'r' in New England ("pahk" for park, "heah" for here) and dropping of the closing 'g' in some parts of the South ("fixin'" for fixing, "goin'" for going). Failing to correctly pronounce a key term is seriously damaging to a speaker's credibility. Make sure you know how to pronounce all the words in your speech, and look up any for which you are not sure of the correct pronunciation. Your **volume** is guided, foremost, by the size of your audience and speaking space. Make sure everyone can hear you clearly throughout the room, then consider when you could increase or decrease your volume to add emphasis or intensity. **Fluency** is often influenced by the rate of your delivery. When you increase your rate, you also increase the likelihood of stumbling over a word, not **articulating** clearly, or mispronouncing a term. It may sound contradictory, but trying to speak too quickly can also increase verbal fillers, those "uhhs" "ummms" and "likes" that creep in when your brain lags behind your lips. Verbal fillers are sometimes called **vocalized pauses**. These are to be avoided. **Pauses** are related to fluency — they're like antidotes to a rate that's too fast, and they should be silent. Pauses can be used for many reasons in a speech — they add emphasis, give you time to think through your next words, and give your audience time to process what you've said. If you lose your place, taking a short, silent pause of up to 15 seconds to check your notes or mentally review what you've said and what you want to say next won't hurt your effectiveness with your audience. In fact, most of them won't even notice a short pause. Planned pauses are great markers of important points. Because our culture is so saturated with noise, a pause can direct attention to an idea in a way that additional speech can't. Consider a slightly extended pause after particularly important or challenging information to let your audience fully comprehend what you've said.

Finding the Authentic Voice

What's most important about your voice when you speak is that it conveys your sincere interest in your topic and your audience. If your voice sounds like you're bored or uninterested in what you're saying, your audience will hear that and tune you out. Why should they care if you don't? On the other hand, even if your topic isn't the most dynamic, if your voice expresses interest and energy, your audience will listen to you and what you have to say. Remember you want to talk *with* them, not *at* them.

Practicing Your Speech - Five Steps

The following five steps all work together to prepare you to speak fluently, confidently, and with positive energy. Each step in the process builds in a key element of effective presentation, so that when you've completed the five steps, you are truly ready to deliver your speech. It's strongly encouraged that you do each of the steps at least once. As you follow the five steps, you may decide that repeating a step helps you feel more comfortable and confident.

Step 1. Sit in a comfortable place, preferably without distractions, with your speech outline or preliminary speaking notes. Go over the structure of the speech out loud. You are NOT giving your speech word for word in this step. You are checking and practicing the organization of the speech to see if it works and if you are comfortable with it. For example, while sitting with your outline, you would say OUT LOUD:

> "I will start with the joke about the chicken. Then I will state how this topic is relevant to my audience. I will make my thesis statement and give my three preview points, X, Y, and Z. I will use another chicken story as a transition to my first main point, X. In my first point, my subpoints are P and Q. I have evidence from source M and source N to support P. More evidence from source M also supports Q, and I have an additional source L for that subpoint."

Go through your entire speech structure in this way. As you are doing so, make notes on your outline to indicate where it flows well or where you feel a bit hesitant or awkward. Note whether you are missing any evidence or if the evidence doesn't sufficiently support your points. When you are finished, consider if any changes need to be made, new evidence included, points moved, or where you need to be more familiar with your material. When you have those changes in place, move on to Step 2.

Step 2. Stand with your revised notes and, again, go through the structure of your speech speaking out loud. The purpose of step 1 was to identify the places where content was missing or changes needed to be made in your overall organization. In this step, you will review the changes from the perspective of your delivery style. For step 2, try to go through the entire speech with a minimal number of stops. If you notice a change that needs to be made, note it and keep going. You are using this step to check any changes from step 1, and also to build your familiarity with the 'feel' of the speech as it is delivered. By the time you are done with step 2, your speech should be very close to its final form, and you should be ready to deliver it with very few full stops.

Step 3. For this step, you need a draft of your speaking notes and room to move. You should be very familiar with the structure and content of your speech by now. In Step 3, deliver the entire speech — not the structure — in plain language and with movement (if you plan to move during your speech). Do your best to get through it without stopping, but if you need to, stop and check the structure or your familiarity with the content. Step 3 is your rough rehearsal; you simply want to get through the speech from beginning to end so you know that you can. If you hesitate, if you stumble over words, if you have to stop and check your notes, that's fine. Just keep going from where you needed to check, and repeat Step 3 until you can get through the entire speech with no more than 5 stops. Then you're ready for Step 4.

Step 4. "Mirror, mirror, on the wall." You will want to be able to see yourself for Step 4. In Step 3 you became familiar with the physical part of delivering your speech with a minimal number of stops. In Step 4, you will deliver your entire speech from beginning to end with NO stops while watching and timing yourself. You need a mirror and whatever limited speaking notes you are allowed for your presentation. If you hesitate, stumble, have "Umms" and "uhhs," or forget what you meant to say, that's okay. But you have to keep going until you reach the end *without* checking anything other than the notes you will use. The mirror helps you to see what your gestures look like, where you tend to make eye contact, and when it seems appropriate to move. It also gives you a little sense of having an audience. Step 4 is where you check the language of your speech. Are there places where you tend to say "Umm," or can you change a word to make it more vivid and compelling? Keep in mind you are your own worst critic, so be kind. Repeat Step 4 until you can deliver the entire speech with only your presentation notes within your allotted time.

Step 5. This is your dress rehearsal step. In Step 5, you will deliver your speech in as close to your final form as you can, to an actual audience, even if that is only one person. Before you start, tell the audience that you would like two kinds of feedback from them—one thing that you did well in the speech, and one thing you could change to make it better. Giving these directions will help them give you useful, constructive feedback. Then give your speech as if it were your presentation day. Make sure you time yourself if you have a time limit. When you are done, ask the audience for their feedback, and consider their response to the speech. Review the entire speech from beginning to end, including where you moved, what gestures you made, and how you did with your vocal delivery. By the time you get to step 5, you are polishing your presentation. You should be so familiar with the content and organization that it's nearly automatic. In step 5, you can work on details of your physical delivery and gauge your effectiveness on your audience.

Figure 13.3 - **Five Steps in Practicing Your Speech**

1. Go over speech structure out loud—identify places where content is lacking

2. Stand and go through speech again, incorporating changes

3. Deliver entire speech with plain language using movement

4. Deliver entire speech from Start to Finish. Time yourself and stand in front of a mirror

5. Do a dress rehearsal—deliver speech as close as possible to its final form in front of an audience

Now you're ready to present, and hopefully your speech is at least a day or so away. As with any performance, taking care of your physical self is important for doing your best. So get a good night's sleep, drink plenty of water (in most cases, it's perfectly okay to bring a water bottle to your presentation), and take time to do your power pose and breathing before you present. Lastly, make sure you have eaten a good meal so that you have the fuel to deliver your best possible speech. Proteins are better choices than carbohydrates. Balancing protein and complex carbohydrates is a much better choice than a meal of simple carbohydrates.

Murphy's Law states that anything that can go wrong, will. When you put in the time to outline and practice your speech, you can drastically reduce the exposure to Murphy's Law: Less can go wrong when you are well prepared. If you have followed the five steps and the other guides for effective presentations in this chapter, you're thoroughly prepared.

Conclusion

In this chapter we have discussed how to prepare for your speech by fine-tuning your preparation outline and converting it into a speaking outline. We also discussed physical delivery, appearance, and vocal quality so you now know exactly **how** you present your speech can support **what** you have to say. Practicing your delivery will improve both the how and the what of your speech, help your audience understand your message, and increase your confidence as a speaker. The Five Steps will guide you through the process of tying all of your preparation together and bringing your best speaking self to your presentation in order to share your ideas with confidence and pride.

Index